Praise for RV H

"New adopters of the lifestyle will join the ranks of happy readers as they learn even more exciting tips and tricks as they enjoy their RV. A copy of *RV Hacks* should be in every RV on the road today."

–Bob Zagami, executive director of New England RV Dealers Association

"*RV Hacks* is full of insights that most RVers could spend years trying to figure out! A huge asset in any RVer's library."

–Cherie Ve Ard & Chris Dunphy of Technomadia.com

"Another home run for this dynamic duo! The hacks in this book are great for all levels of RV experience, and so much fun to read you can't put the book down."

–Sandy Ellingson, RV industry consultant

"The hacks and tricks contained within this book will save you countless hours of trial and error—and money—and make your journey in an RV so much more enjoyable!"

–Mark Koep, founder and CEO of CampgroundViews.com

"The Bennetts' newest book is simply a must-have for every RV traveler who is looking to enjoy the journey with a little less stress and a lot more adventure."

–Jeff Shelton, CEO and owner of Wholesale Warranties

"Marc and Julie's *RV Hacks* is jam-packed with need-to-know tips, tricks, and hacks for your RV travels that will keep you on the road longer!"

–Nicole Sult, senior director of customer experience, Lippert Components

"You're going to want to dig into this book for hundreds of handy hacks that you might never have thought of—it will help you enjoy your RV lifestyle all the more!"

–Rick Kessler, executive editor of *RVBusiness*

Praise for *RV Hacks*

"I wish I had read a book like this before I started RVing; it would have saved me countless hours and helped me plan the best trips possible!"

–Andy Robinowitz, CEO of RV LIFE

"*RV Hacks* provides hacks and tips for everyday situations that may come up—or just hacks to make your RV experience even better!"

–Sean Nichols, COO of Battle Born Batteries

"The Bennetts' new book is an encyclopedia of tips from RVers all over North America, continuing a long-standing tradition of RVers sharing things that help them on the road. A lot of great hacks that RVers old and new will appreciate and enjoy."

–Chris Dougherty, technical director of *RV Enthusiast*

"Marc and Julie are like those trusted friends you know you can always count on to share invaluable tips and insights; their *RV Hacks* will help you navigate through it all and enjoy the journey."

–Sarah Smith, CVO and cofounder of The Dyrt

"Marc and Julie Bennett's latest book, *RV Hacks*, is a breath of fresh air, jam-packed with great RV experience and insight."

–Larry McNamara, CEO and owner of Giant Recreation World

"*RV Hacks* is really a book for everyone. A great read…wisdom and fun for all. If RVing is important to you—not the mechanics, but the whole RV lifestyle—it is an absolute must."

–John Sztykiel, cofounder of No Dirty Earth

"*RV Hacks* is the rare how-to book that has you wanting to do everything in it! The tips and tricks within will genuinely save any RV owner loads of time and money. Bravo to the Bennetts!"

–Jason and Abby Epperson of the *RV Miles* podcast

RV HACKS

RV HACKS

400+ WAYS TO MAKE LIFE ON THE ROAD
EASIER, SAFER, *and More Fun!*

MARC AND JULIE BENNETT Bestselling Authors of *Living the RV Life*

ADAMS MEDIA

NEW YORK   LONDON   TORONTO   SYDNEY   NEW DELHI

Adams Media
An Imprint of Simon & Schuster, Inc.
100 Technology Center Drive
Stoughton, Massachusetts 02072

First Adams Media trade paperback edition July 2021

ADAMS MEDIA and colophon are trademarks of Simon & Schuster.

For information about special discounts for bulk purchases, please contact Simon & Schuster Special Sales at 1-866-506-1949 or business@simonandschuster.com.

The Simon & Schuster Speakers Bureau can bring authors to your live event. For more information or to book an event contact the Simon & Schuster Speakers Bureau at 1-866-248-3049 or visit our website at www.simonspeakers.com.

Interior design by Colleen Cunningham
Cover photographs © Julie Bennett, Brandy Reneau
Interior photograph credits listed alongside photos
Interior illustrations © Eric Andrews; 123RF/Pivden, filborg, Liudmyla Pushnova, joingate; Getty Images/appleuzr

Manufactured in the United States of America

10 9 8 7 6 5

Library of Congress Cataloging-in-Publication Data
Names: Bennett, Marc, author. | Bennett, Julie, author.
Title: RV hacks / Marc and Julie Bennett, bestselling authors of Living the RV life.
Other titles: Recreational vehicle hacks
Description: First Adams Media trade paperback edition. | Stoughton, Massachusetts: Adams Media, 2021. | Includes index.
Identifiers: LCCN 2021013676 | ISBN 9781507216576 (pb) | ISBN 9781507216583 (ebook)
Subjects: LCSH: Recreational vehicle living--Miscellanea.
Classification: LCC TX1110 .B453 2021 | DDC 910--dc23
LC record available at https://lccn.loc.gov/2021013676

ISBN 978-1-5072-1657-6
ISBN 978-1-5072-1658-3 (ebook)

DEDICATION

For all you RVers...young or old, newbie or seasoned,
driving motorhomes or towing campers. Whether you're
out living the dream or you find yourself trying to figure
out a solution to the conundrums of life on the road,
remember: It's all part of the adventure. We wrote this
book for you so you can feel confident in the knowledge
that no matter what RV life throws at you, you've got this!

CONTENTS

◄ *Previous spread: State Route 1, California / Photo © Julie Bennett*

INTRODUCTION

Whether you're camping just down the road or exploring part of the country hundreds or thousands of miles from you, an RV can bring you amazing adventures, a sense of freedom, and so many great experiences. But, like with any type of travel, things can go wrong once in a while. Don't worry—*RV Hacks* is here to help prevent and fix those headaches! In these pages, we've collected more than four hundred quick and easy hacks to help improve every aspect of your RV life and travels. You'll save time and money, make your trip safer, and ensure your whole trip runs as smoothly as possible.

Since 2014, we have been living, breathing, and sleeping the RV lifestyle 24/7 after hitting the road full-time in our RV. We've invented and collected hundreds of hacks along the way—with the goal of improving our own RV life, and yours! As we wrote this book, we also reached out to more than two dozen of our favorite RVers (and perhaps yours too?) for their useful advice since they, too, have been there, done that, and lived to tell the tale!

This book is packed with creative solutions for tackling just about every aspect of RV living. For example:

- Nervous about driving that large vehicle? Flip to Chapter 1 for tips on how to improve your skills without risking damage to your RV.
- Terrified of a sewer tank disaster? In Chapter 2, you'll learn everything you need to stay calm and clean and dump your tanks like a pro.

- Wondering where to find the best campsites? Chapter 3 recommends a list of websites and apps to help you uncover hidden gems.
- Overwhelmed by how to fit all your stuff in your RV? Get tips and tricks for organization and storage in Chapter 4.
- Unsure how to connect to the Internet while you roam? Find solutions for all things technology and work related in Chapter 5.
- Worried about traveling with pets or kids? Head to Chapter 6 for tips and tools for keeping *all* members of your traveling party busy, happy, and healthy.

Whatever problems you're facing, this book has the tips, tools, and answers to get you through them.

You can start at the beginning, jump to the chapter where you need the most help, or randomly flip to any page for a quick tip. Keep this book in your RV as you travel so you can find handy solutions to common problems and learn to RV like a pro. Buckle up, and let's get on the road!

PS: Find more hacks, discounts, and links—and even submit a hack of your own—at RVLove.com/BonusHacks.

ACKNOWLEDGMENTS

This book comes at a time when more people than ever before are getting the chance to discover what's so great about the RV life. And while the open road, freedom to travel, and places you can see are incredible, you know what is the best thing about RV life? The people. You won't find a more resourceful, helpful, and generous group of folks anywhere else.

Before we even started RVing full-time back in 2014, we learned so much from those who had been RVing for years and decades before us. We've learned even more through our own firsthand experience on the road, coming up with unique solutions to our problems. And we continue to learn from the handy, creative, and often ingenious solutions we discover while walking around campgrounds, perusing various sources online, and sharing stories with friends over campfires.

Many hacks are learned through self-reliance, while trying to get ourselves out of a pickle. Something RVers learn to do pretty quickly is think on their feet and find a way to fix things themselves. Being self-reliant and willing to take on a DIY project—even if you need a blog post or *YouTube* video to walk you through it—will take you far.

Our *RVLove* community is made up of more than one hundred thousand of these amazing, knowledgeable, and helpful individuals. That includes the more than two dozen highly experienced RVers who contributed to this book, simply because they wanted to help make the road smoother for you.

A huge, heartfelt thank you to the following people:

- Dennis and Donna Baril **(Hacks 18, 75, 290)**
- Brett and Danelle Hays **(Hack 253)**
- Mike and Anne Howard of HoneyTrek.com and authors of *Ultimate Journeys for Two* and *Comfortably Wild* **(Hack 276)**
- Peter Knize and John Sullivan of TheRVGeeks.com and hosts of *The RVers* TV show **(Hacks 117, 280)**
- Mark Koep of CampgroundViews.com **(Hacks 50, 68, 134, 136, 138)**
- Duane Lipham of RVInspectionandCare.com **(Hacks 24, 84, 85, 87, 126, 286, 287)**
- Erik and Kala McCauley of LivinLite.net and MobileMustHave.com **(Hacks 59, 129, 233, 347, 349, 414)**
- Caitlin and Tom Morton of MortonsontheMove.com **(Hack 386)**
- Marissa and Nathan Moss of LessJunkMoreJourney .com **(Hacks 265, 266, 374)**
- Heath and Alyssa Padgett of HeathandAlyssa .com; host of *The RV Entrepreneur* podcast (Heath) and author of *A Beginner's Guide to Living in an RV* (Alyssa) **(Hacks 301, 306, 310, 346, 378, 379)**
- Janine Pettit of GirlCamper.com and Editor in Chief of *Girl Camper* magazine **(Hack 35)**
- Stephanie and Jeremy Puglisi of *The RV Atlas* podcast and authors of *See You at the Campground* and *Where Should We Camp Next?* **(Hacks 364, 369–371)**
- Brian and Melissa Pursel of RVwithTito.com **(Hacks 124, 128, 130)**
- Jim and Brandy Reneau **(Hack 387)**
- Tim and Emily Rohrer of OwnLessDoMore.us **(Hacks 82, 288)**

- Bryanna Royal of CrazyFamilyAdventure.com and author of *Full-Time RVing with Kids* (**Hack 363**)
- Kali and Josh Spiers of *The Freedom Theory* on *YouTube* (**Hack 357**)
- Ken and Helen Storr (**Hacks 65, 148, 194**)
- Cherie Ve Ard and Chris Dunphy of Technomadia .com and RVMobileInternet.com (**Hacks 147, 333, 336, 338-343**)
- Juliet Whitfield of TailsfromtheRoad.com (**Hacks 22, 90, 382, 389, 391, 400, 408-413**)
- Christine and Aaron Willers of IreneIronFitness .com (**Hacks 225, 226, 229, 248-251, 274**)

You'll find even more of their wisdom and content online, so check them out! Some of these awesome RVers are also featured in our first book, *Living the RV Life: Your Ultimate Guide to Life on the Road.* What can we say...you all rock!

High fives to our RV industry connections and friends, and our publishing team at Simon & Schuster/Adams Media, in particular Cate Coulacos Prato and Laura Daly.

Finally, a pat on the back to *you* for taking the time to read this. Most people skip right past the Acknowledgments. We hope you love the book and are able to put some of these RV hacks into action right away to make your RVing adventures even better!

Best of *life*,

Marc and Julie Bennett

of RVLove.com and authors of *Living the RV Life*

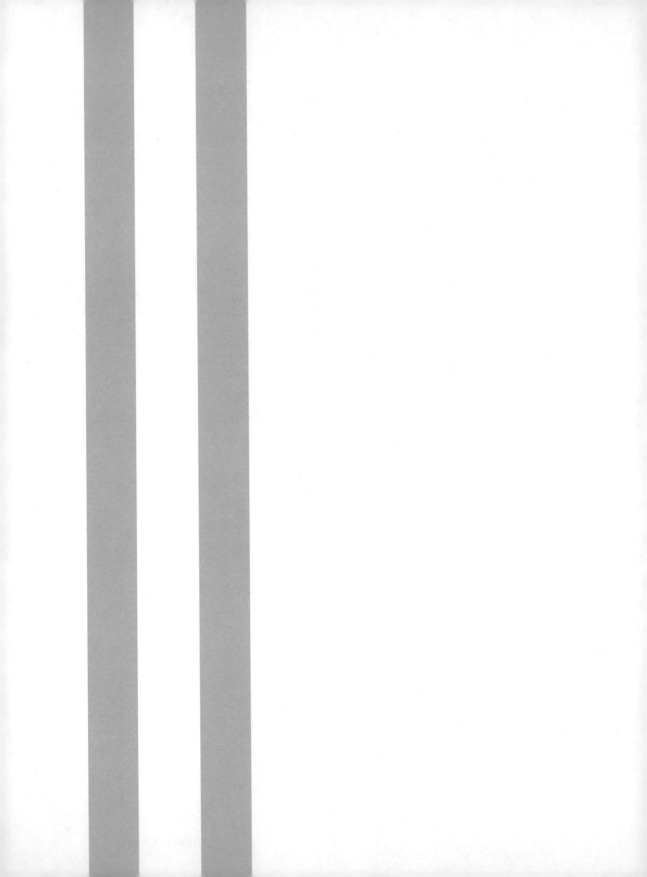

Chapter 1
DRIVING

Hitting the open road in an RV is really exciting, whether it's your first time or your fiftieth! Whether you're towing a small trailer or driving a large motorhome, here are our best hacks for planning your trip, improving your gas mileage, and reaching your destination safe and sound.

Allow time and space for serendipity and surprises along the way.

1 Plan your route in advance.

Spend time planning your route before you get behind the wheel so you are familiar with the route and the best roads to take. This can save you time on travel days and ensure a safer and less stressful drive. The larger the RV, the more important advance trip planning becomes, since the consequences are higher and it's not as easy to get out of a tricky situation! Proper planning and preparation pay off—literally!

2 Don't overplan your trip.

Allow time and space for serendipity and surprises along the way. If you are too rigid in your planning, you lose the ability to adapt or accept unexpected invitations and opportunities.

3 Use rest stops responsibly.

Find rest stops using the USA Rest Stops app or AllStays Pro app, then stay out of the way of truckers who need to stop and rest. They don't have other options for parking at campgrounds like the rest of us.

4 Stop for breaks at state parks.

If you're looking for somewhere to stop and visit, make a pit stop and take an extended lunch break at a local state park, and park in their public parking lot. Admission is usually under $10 per vehicle—many are free—and if it's a state you drive through or visit often, it may be worth getting an annual state park pass. Some state parks are more RV friendly than others and tend to be popular, so check their website for more information.

◀ *Blue Mesa Reservoir, Colorado / Photo © Marc Bennett*

Ten Best Ways to Plan Your RV Route

5 Carry these essential paper books.

For excellent guidance when doing RV route planning, use highly recommended print resources like the latest edition of *Road Atlas* (by Rand McNally), *The Next Exit*, *Mountain Directory East*, and *Mountain Directory West* and keep them in your RV. Having print books will come in handy if you don't have Internet access or your phone battery dies.

6 Get an RV-specific GPS unit.

Invest in an RV-specific GPS and program it with your RV height, weight, length, and number of propane tanks. It will provide more accuracy and safety than Google Maps or Apple Maps (both designed for cars). No GPS is perfect, so use it but don't trust it blindly. You still need to pay attention to road signs along the way.

7 Use an online trip planner with RV-safe GPS.

Plan your trip with a useful online tool like RVTrip Wizard.com, which uses your RV-specific data to help you plan RV-friendly routes, find campgrounds, plan fuel stops, and track your trip budget. Then access your trip via the RV LIFE app on your smart device to follow step-by-step RV-safe GPS directions.

8 Find free overnight parking.

Break up long drives at free overnight parking locations where it is allowed. Find them using the AllStays app (pay for the pro version—it's worth it!) with the overnight free parking filter turned on to find Walmart parking lots, truck stops, Cracker Barrel and Cabela's locations that may allow you to stay.

9 Download your route for offline use.

Cell coverage isn't guaranteed, so download a planned travel route onto your smartphone or tablet so you can follow RV-safe directions, even in areas with spotty or zero cell signal.

10 Use Google Satellite and Street View features.

Use these tools to get familiar with the terrain you'll be traveling and to check the parking options as well as the entry and exit points of gas stations, campgrounds, and other stops before you go. This tip is especially important for big rigs.

11 Read websites and use apps.

Use online tools such as AllStays, *Big Rigs Best Bets*, Campendium, Campground Reviews.com, Campground Views.com, RV LIFE, Togo RV, and The Dyrt to read up on peer-reviewed RV parks and campgrounds.

12 Check the weather.

Use services like the NOAA Weather Radar Live app and Weather High-Def Radar app to track inclement weather in the days before your trip and make adjustments to your itinerary or route as needed, to avoid high winds and storms.

13 Mix up your travels.

Seek out unique overnight stays at casinos through CasinoCamper.com. Stay at farms, wineries, and golf clubs through programs like Harvest Hosts. Camp for free on private host properties at *Boondockers Welcome*. Find and book unique outdoor stays through Hipcamp.

14 Discover interesting attractions.

Use apps like Roadtrippers, The Dyrt, and RV LIFE to find attractions and plan ahead for scenic lunch spots and bathroom breaks. Take your time and enjoy the journey!

15   Allow more time for RV road trips.

Don't plan your ETA around what Google Maps suggests. Road trips by RV almost always take longer than road trips by car for multiple reasons. RVs are typically slower to drive and maneuver, and driving them is more taxing mentally and physically, as you need to really focus. You're also more likely to stop for meals, bathroom breaks, and roadside attractions—simply because you can. And because you're taking your vacation home with you, the drive itself is often the entertainment. So plan at least an extra 20 percent of time for RV road trip ETAs, or more if your goal is to take in the sights along the way and not simply drive from home to your destination and back.

16   Use Google Maps only for initial route planning.

Google Maps is designed for passenger vehicles, not RVs! It can be handy for doing initial trip planning—the Satellite and Street View functions are useful and also help you find some stops along your way—and it can be a handy backup, but don't rely on it as your primary navigation tool unless you have a very small RV. Don't try to take shortcuts, or you'll learn the hard way.

17   Remember that bigger isn't always better.

Whether you're renting or buying an RV, choose the smallest one you feel you and your travel companions can be comfortable in. The larger the RV, the more limiting it will be to drive, and the more difficult it will be to find places to park it. It's not impossible, but it does require more planning and flexibility. For example, you can usually find campsites for large RVs in campgrounds located within 5–20 miles of most national parks, but if you really want to camp inside these popular parks, you'll have much better luck finding a site and navigating interior roads with a smaller RV.

18 **Use two GPS units when driving big rigs to offer different route options.**

If you have a big rig, it can really pay off to have more than one opinion on the best route to follow. GPS units have different data and software, and therefore provide different recommendations.

DENNIS AND DONNA BARIL

"We were thrilled when we bought our first Class A motorhome to see an RV GPS in the dashboard. We were assured that our rig's weight and dimensions were used to calculate routes, thereby avoiding bridges, tunnels, and roads that we should not travel. That's why we were surprised when just a few weeks later we were on a potholed dirt road with trees hanging all ready to scratch and damage our rig. After unhitching our car and slowly backing out, we knew we needed a better solution. We decided to buy an RV GPS manufactured by a different company. The second GPS often leads us on different routes or portions of routes. We quickly realized the algorithm was different in each unit and neither was best all the time. On one short day trip, one unit chose a 175-mile route and the other chose a 325-mile route! Over the years, we've learned to appreciate the difference, and we use Google Maps (which does not route using RV weight and dimensions) or the old standard—paper maps—to review and determine why any conflicts exist and what is the best route to travel. Since that first experience, in 5 years of full-time travel, we've never had to disconnect the car along our route."

19

Decide whether to toll, or not to toll.

Toll roads charge by axle, and unlike passenger cars and trucks, many RVs have more than two axles! RV tolls can easily be two to four times the price of tolls for regular vehicles. Plan ahead and decide if a toll road is worth taking or not. If the toll road saves a lot of miles, it could be worth it in fuel economy savings, as most RVs get poor fuel mileage. Plus, if you're pressed for time, the toll road might get you there faster. But you can often save on toll charges by taking an alternate—and perhaps more scenic—route to your destination. Use a toll calculator app to help you estimate toll charges. Keep in mind these toll rates are generally for cars, so pad the cost for RVs. You can also set your GPS or navigation app to avoid tolls, where possible.

20 Save money at the pump.

Use apps and join RV-friendly fuel programs to locate the best fuel prices in your area. Apps like GasBuddy (for all fuel types) and Mudflap and the TSD Logistics fuel program for RVers (for diesel fuel) can help you save big. Just use Google Street View to make sure you can access the gas station with your RV.

21 Check your pre-travel checklist before driving.

Create and follow a pre-travel checklist specific to your RV setup as you pack everything up on departure days, and make sure you've covered everything before you put the RV into drive. Print and laminate a list that you can wipe clean for your next trip. Or create a digital version with boxes you can check off each time.

22 Sail through cities by avoiding peak traffic.

Driving an RV through a city can be so challenging because of the traffic. But planning your timing will remove stress from your city drive. Make your trip through the heart of the city between 10 a.m. and 2 p.m., preferably closer to noon, by driving the interstate that goes right through the middle of the city. Generally, you should encounter less traffic.

23 Learn to drive an RV with a moving truck.

If you have never driven a large vehicle before, rent a moving truck before buying, renting, or driving an RV. You'll get a feel for what it's like to drive and navigate a large vehicle on roads and through traffic. It's inexpensive, less complicated, and more durable—just make sure it is covered by insurance! It's an easy way to gain confidence driving a bigger vehicle before hitting the road in an RV.

24 Follow the rule of 3-3-3 to reduce stress and fatigue.

For low-stress travel days and safe arrivals, adopt and follow the rule of 3-3-3 that many experienced RVers swear by. 1) Don't travel more than 3 days in a row without stopping for a few days' rest. 2) Try not to drive more than 300 miles in any one day. 3) Arrive at your destination before 3 p.m. Some RVers may prefer to follow a similar 2-2-2 rule, but either one will work, depending on your preferred driving style and pace.

DUANE LIPHAM OF RVINSPECTIONANDCARE.COM

"Driving motorhomes or towing an RV for long distances can be both physically and mentally taxing. Before we started RVing, I learned that many experienced RVers reduce their travel stress and anxiety by practicing the 3-3-3 rule. I've been following this practice for a few years now, and it's never let me down. I have found it keeps my road stress and anxiety to a minimum, and also ensures we don't arrive at our campsite in the dark, which makes it easier and safer to set up camp."

25 Scout out boondocking locations ahead of time in your regular vehicle.

If you are planning on camping in your RV on open land without hookups (also known as *boondocking*), scout out the area in advance with your towed or towing vehicle to ensure the road is suitable and safe to bring your RV on. Look out for narrow roads, deep ruts, low-hanging trees, and low clearance. Even if you've been there before, conditions can change over time or become wet and muddy. Many roadside assistance tow trucks may not be willing to drive into remote roads to get you out, so confirm you can access a road before driving in with your RV.

26 Understand mile markers and exits.

Exit numbers on most interstate highways are aligned with numbered mile markers—and these reset when entering a new state. So, if you know what number exit you need to get off at, you can quickly estimate how many miles to your destination. For example, if you are at mile marker 60, and you need to exit at mile marker 75, you know you have 15 miles to go. Know whether your upcoming exit will be on the left or right side by paying attention to the position of the tabs on top of the exit signs. As you travel the country, you'll find right exits are more common, but you'll come across left exits from time to time.

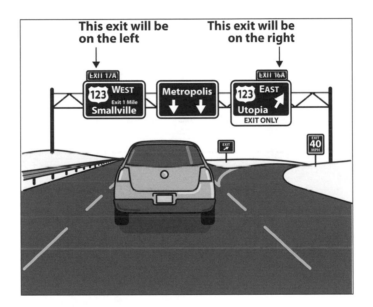

27 Use your towed vehicle as a trailer.

If you need to carry a bit of extra cargo for your trip but you don't have the spare cargo carrying capacity (CCC) in your RV, put the heavier items in your towed vehicle, effectively using it as a trailer. This will help disperse the weight and avoid making the RV overweight, which increases your safety.

28   Maximize your fuel economy.

You will get much better fuel economy when you drive between 55 and 60 mph. Most RVs (and trucks) are large and will be impacted by frictional and aerodynamic drag, which both affect your fuel economy. Save on fuel costs by sticking to a safe speed limit of no more than 60 mph. If they are suitable for your RV, take back roads and scenic highways instead of inter-states and freeways. These types of roads and slower speeds are not only safer and less stressful, but will also be more enjoyable and relaxing while saving you money.

29   Read road signs to stay safe.

Never rely *solely* on your GPS. Road conditions change, some-times with very short notice, and GPS units are not foolproof. They are only as good as the data they have, and the data is not always current. Keep on top of GPS software and map updates. And always keep an eye out for signs like this one.

30   Watch, learn from, and follow truckers.

Pay attention to the driving habits of professional truck drivers—such as the lanes they choose and where they exit. Most have driven those roads many times, and they also stay in communication with other professional drivers, so they often know what's up ahead. Truckers will likely be choosing lanes best suited for large vehicles, so it may make sense for you to follow them, especially if you're driving or towing a large RV.

31   Turn off propane before driving.

Be safe and reduce damage to your equipment while driving by turning off propane at the tank before driving your RV. When the propane is in operation, it has an open flame—a bad idea when visiting a fuel station. But you also want to avoid having your propane fridge running while the RV is in motion, especially if driving over hills, mountains, or steep grades (use ice to keep your food cold while the propane is off). Operating an RV fridge when it is not level can cause damage to the fridge over time, potentially causing a malfunction or even a fire. Many newer RVs are switching to residential-style fridges, and these can be left on while driving if you have enough battery power or run the generator.

32 Know and display the height and weight of your RV.

Check your RV's height, length, and weight and post them on your RV windshield or dash for easy reference. That way when you're approaching bridges, tunnels, and smaller roads, you'll quickly know whether your RV can safely travel on them or you need to find an alternate route. Always add at least a few extra inches to your actual RV height (including rooftop air conditioners, antennas, etc.) before driving under bridges or in tunnels. Over time, as roads are resurfaced, the extra layers of asphalt can reduce the actual safe height available for vehicles driving under them.

33 Travel during business hours to access mechanical support.

Plan to drive your RV during regular business hours, if possible. If you break down or a system stops working, you can more easily find support and avoid an after-hours surcharge. Sometimes a simple phone call to a repair shop, your RV dealer, or your RV manufacturer during regular working hours can get you the fix or information you need to get back on the road quickly. RV roadside assistance is a good thing to have—just know that, depending on the issue, you may not always be able to get the level of help you need after hours.

34   Find your center in the lane so you drive safely.

When driving a large vehicle or RV, staying centered in your lane is both more important and more difficult than in a car or passenger truck. With your copilot's help, establish when you are centered in a lane—at a stop sign, for example. Place a dot sticker or piece of blue tape on the windshield to mark a spot aligned visually in the foreground. That will help you line up the dot with a lane divider or the side of the road, providing a consistent, easy visual reference until it becomes second nature.

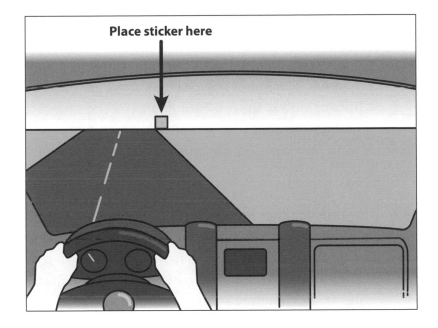

Place sticker here

35 Practice towing with a U-Haul trailer.

If you have never towed or backed up a trailer, rent a trailer from a moving company like U-Haul and practice in a parking lot before renting or buying an RV. It's a cheap and low-risk way to get your skills and confidence up before hitting the road with your RV! The rental trailer should be covered by insurance (check!), and you won't run the risk of damaging your own RV.

JANINE PETTIT OF GIRLCAMPER.COM AND EDITOR IN CHIEF OF *GIRL CAMPER* MAGAZINE

"People write to me saying they are scared to tow and asking for advice. Towing is a learned skill set, no different than riding a bike or skiing. Start by going on *YouTube* to watch videos about how to tow. U-Haul actually has really good videos about how to tow. If you know someone experienced with towing, ask if you can ride along with them and have them show you. The more experienced person can explain what they look for when they are driving—for example, why they might choose one lane or another in given situations. Next, rent a U-Haul trailer. They are only about $20 for a 1-day rental. They will probably even hook it up to your towing vehicle for you. Keep in mind if it was dangerous, insurance companies would not let unskilled people rent trailers! Those trailers are small, lightweight, empty, and durable: perfect for learning. Schedule a time when all the school buses are off the road. Drive around your hometown on roads you are familiar with first. Drive the side roads, in and out of large parking lots. Then, after driving around and building confidence that the trailer is still back there, get on and off of the highway. Remember that all kinds of people tow trailers every day. Those same people put their pants on one leg at a time, just like you do. You have access to the same special skills that they have—you just need to unearth them."

36

Weigh and balance your RV.

Staying within your RV weight-carrying capacity is not only safer; it also delivers better fuel economy and reduces wear and tear on your RV—all of which will save you money. Get your RV weighed at a truck stop with CAT Scales to accurately weigh your RV and tow vehicle by axle. Better yet, go the extra mile by getting all four corners of your RV weighed at a dedicated weighing location that offers this service (e.g., Escapees SmartWeigh program locations and some RV rallies). To more evenly balance out the weight you're carrying across the axles—or, ideally, all four corners—you'll need to redistribute items inside your RV and storage bays as best you can—or off-load stuff you don't really need.

37 Understand the US highways and interstate numbering system.

North-south interstates are always odd numbers (e.g., I-25), while east-west interstates are even numbers (e.g., I-70). The lowest numbers for north-south interstates start on the west side of the country (e.g., I-5), and the highest number is on the east side (e.g., I-95). The interstates that run east-west across the country start in the southernmost part of the US with the lowest number (e.g., I-10), and the highest number is in the far north (e.g., I-90). Highways and beltways that go around a city have three numbers instead of two (e.g., I-225).

38 Know how much weight you can safely carry.

RV weight is a big deal, and not all RVs of the same size can carry the same amount of weight! Find the maximum safe weight you can carry in your RV by checking the yellow sticker near the entry door or driver area. Find the cargo carrying capacity and deduct the weight of water in your tanks (8.3 pounds per gallon), as well as clothes, food, and other gear. Remember, if you are driving a motorhome, the cargo carrying capacity limit includes the weight of all passengers, including pets, plus fuel. Weight can add up quickly, and staying within the designated weight limit will keep you—and your RV—safer on the road.

MOTOR HOME OCCUPANT AND CARGO CARRYING CAPACITY
VIN# XXXXXXXXXXXXXXXXX
THE COMBINED WEIGHT OF OCCUPANTS AND CARGO SHOULD NEVER EXCEED:
534 kg or 1178 lbs
Safety belt equipped seating capacity: 4
CAUTION:
A full load of water equals 183 kg or 398 lbs of cargo @1kg/L (8.3 lb/gal) and the tongue weight of a towed trailer counts as cargo
(Serial # XXXXXXXXXXXXX)

39 Make fuel filling a breeze.

Before each trip, plan on filling your tow vehicle with fuel before connecting to your trailer. This will provide greater ease in filling by not dealing with the additional length of your RV, and it will offer more selection in fuel prices and locations. If you're traveling in a large RV or motorhome, plan to fill up at truck stops (for diesel) or other RV-friendly locations that offer easier entry and exit points and higher rooftop clearance (e.g., Love's, Pilot Flying J Travel Center, TA-Petro, and Buc-ee's Travel Centers). Some fuel stations even have RV-specific lanes to fill your tank, and may have the option for you to dump waste tanks, fill your fresh water tanks, and/or fill the air in your tires.

40 Turn from the outside lane to make the move easier.

If you encounter more than one turn lane (and don't need to immediately take a left or right), use the outside turning lane. It will give you more room, with a much wider space and more gentle turn angle, which will be especially helpful for larger RVs.

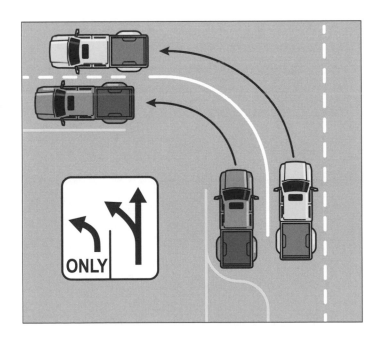

41 Manage your water weight effectively.

Water is heavy, weighing 8.3 pounds per gallon, and can quickly consume your safe RV cargo carrying capacity. Rather than traveling with a full fresh water tank, just carry enough water for a travel day (5–10 gallons should be enough for basic use) and fill your fresh tank when you arrive at—or get close to—your camping destination. Likewise, dump your waste tanks right after your camping trip so you're not carrying that water weight too far. This will increase safety and fuel economy and avoid a stinky mess sloshing around in your tanks and smelling up your RV.

42 Avoid driving on windy days.

High winds are not usually a big factor when driving a car. But RVs have much more surface area per pound of weight, so they can be a greater safety risk when driving in strong winds. It can be hard to predict wind direction. A strong side wind can push you out of your lane or, in extreme situations, even flip you over. A headwind will significantly reduce your fuel economy. In short, driving in winds can be stressful and tiring. Keep an eye on weather apps before and during your trips, and avoid driving on windy days if you can. If unexpected winds kick up and start blowing you around while driving, it can be a good reason to stop to take a break or enjoy a diversion.

▶ *Million Dollar Highway, Colorado / Photo © Julie Bennett*

Use two GPS units
when driving big rigs.

43   Opt for convenient and affordable local rides.

If you don't really need a vehicle for driving and exploring at your destination but you need something with more range and capability than a regular bicycle, save the money you would otherwise spend on an expensive towing setup and car. Instead, rent a car locally or catch an Uber, a Lyft, or a taxi ride. You can get an electric bicycle or even mount a small scooter or moped on a rack behind your motorhome, or carry it in a truck or toy hauler for a more fun and fuel-efficient local ride.

44   Use Tow/Haul mode for better driving mechanics.

Many pickup trucks and motorhomes have a feature on their transmission that allows you to select Tow/Haul mode. This mode provides better towing power by holding gears longer, and also helps assist in braking by downshifting the transmission when applying the brakes. Every transmission works slightly differently, so you may need to read your owner's manual for a more thorough understanding. This feature can increase your safety and driving enjoyment, so if your vehicle has the option, be sure to engage it. If you have a truck and trailer combination, you probably need to use it only when connected. Add this step to your pack-up checklist so you always remember to turn it on.

45 **Store safety gear in a safe location to access.**

Keep your roadside safety gear—emergency lights, safety vest, cones, tools, etc.—stored inside your vehicle or on the curb side of your RV's exterior storage bays. In the event you end up on the side of the road with a breakdown, that's when you'll need safe and easy access, and you don't want to have to do that from the street side, as it's more dangerous with traffic whizzing by.

46 **Calculate your RV tail swing to avoid hitting anything while maneuvering.**

Did you know that the tail of an RV can swing outward approximately 1 foot for every 3 feet of length behind the rear axle? When maneuvering your RV in tight spaces like gas stations and campsites, it can be easy to hit a pole, tree, or other object when making a turn. Calculate your tail swing by measuring the distance between your rear axle to the rear bumper of your RV and dividing by 3. Stay at least that distance away from any object if you know you'll be turning, to maintain a safe clearance. If you are driving a triple-axle RV, measure from the middle axle to the rear of the RV and divide by 3 and maintain at least that distance.

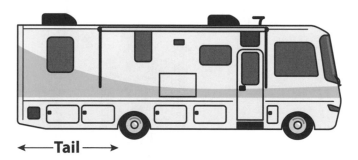
←—**Tail**—→

47   **Get roadside assistance with RV towing.**

Not all roadside assistance programs will cover RVs or the cost of towing if you break down. Towing an RV can be very expensive (hundreds or even thousands of dollars), so get a roadside assistance plan that covers your RV and includes towing too!

48   **Avoid overheating your brakes.**

When you need to use your brakes to slow down, press them firmly for 5–10 seconds—as needed—instead of riding your brakes. Avoid maintaining consistent light pressure on the brake pedal for long periods, as it will create constant friction, which can cause your brakes to overheat and become squishy, and they won't work properly when you need them.

49   **Adjust your rearview mirrors for optimal view.**

When you look in the mirrors, the horizon should be the top third of the view of your main mirror. If you have a curved secondary mirror as well, angle it outward to increase visibility of a vehicle in your blind spot in the next lane.

50 Upgrade your tires and suspension on your RV.

Many used RVs have tires that are old or in poor condition, and many new RVs are sold with tires and suspension components that are near their safe limits right off the factory floor. Upgrading these kinds of components can help avoid breakdowns and/or damage to your RV, and increase your safety.

MARK KOEP OF CAMPGROUNDVIEWS.COM

"When we bought our first RV many years ago, we ended up with multiple flat tires in our first few hundred miles of travel. It was a pre-owned fifth wheel with 3-year-old tires that were in poor condition. We discovered those original tires were also at their maximum weight rating before we even loaded any of our cargo. When we had our first flat tire, we took the RV to a tire shop to replace the whole set of tires. That shop replaced our 3-year-old tires with tires with better weight ratings. But we later learned they were 13-year-old tires! We soon found ourselves with yet another flat. We almost gave up on RVing, but we had already sold everything and our RV was our home! After replacing that second full set of aged-out tires, we got a fast education on the importance of RV tires and what our trailer was riding on. We purchased a brand-new set of tires that were rated well above the weight we were carrying. Yes, we learned the hard way. But if you're buying (or own) a towable RV, the first items that need to be replaced and upgraded are the tires and suspension components. Many RV manufacturers skimp on these things, so it is critical that you immediately upgrade. For rims and tires, I use pickup truck–graded rims with LT (Light Truck) tires. For suspension components, you want, at a minimum, the heaviest-duty bolts, bushings, and equalizers you can install. That's our standard practice now—and we have since towed our RV more than 60,000 miles over the last 11 years of full-time RVing with zero failures."

51

Slow down to save money.

What's the rush? Slow down and take your time; you may enjoy yourself more and end up saving money too! A slower pace of travel saves you money in multiple ways—driving slower means better fuel economy; driving fewer miles uses less fuel; and campground rates are often better for longer stays of a week, month, or more. Plus, you'll spend less time setting up and breaking down camp to move, and you'll have the time to pick up more tips from the locals on the best gems to visit. Less touristy places are less expensive and less crowded too.

52 **Be ready to answer the "Are we there yet?" question.**

When you are driving on a highway at 60 mph, you are basically traveling a mile each minute. So when you get the inevitable question of how long it will be until you arrive at your destination, you can give a good estimate by converting the remaining miles into minutes.

53 **Highlight roads traveled in an atlas to remind yourself later where you went.**

Mark the roads you drive in your RV with a different-colored highlighter for each year to keep track and revisit your travels and routes taken. This helps you remember those roads for next time and know if you want to revisit them or take a different route.

54 **Disconnect a towed car on steep grades to increase safety.**

If you're approaching a long steep grade while driving a motorhome and towed car combination and are concerned about RV brakes and safety, consider pulling over and disconnecting your tow vehicle so your copilot (if you have one) can drive the pass (up or down) separately. You won't put the RV under as much strain, and you'll be able to tackle the mountain at a more reasonable speed, as the weight of a tow vehicle can slow you down. The time it takes to unhook and reconnect will be offset by your new driving time, plus you will increase your safety and reduce your stress, while saving your brakes.

55 Downshift gears before tackling steep grades.

Downshift your transmission to a lower gear before you start going down the hill, not during the descent. Plan on using the same gear you would need to climb that hill. So if you need to downshift to first or second gear to climb a hill, you will want to also use first or second gear when descending a hill that is similarly steep.

56 Pick the best driving lane.

When three driving lanes are available in a metropolitan area, it is generally best to be in the center lane. You will encounter fewer obstacles (like low-hanging tree branches), and there will be fewer vehicles entering and exiting the lanes. On smaller highways, you will generally want to drive in the slow lane to help the flow of traffic and stick to a safe speed, as RV tires are not usually rated for high speed.

57 Increase your front curb-side tire pressure slightly to reduce tire wear.

When driving a motorhome with large high-pressure tires, try adding an extra 2–3 extra pounds of air pressure on the front curb-side tire compared to the front street-side tire. Most highways and roadways are slightly angled for better drainage, and this slight increase in tire pressure can allow your RV to hold its line better on the road, and it can actually reduce some of your tire wear. This is common practice among many professional truck drivers and can apply to large RVs too.

58 Predict handling of a motorhome before driving it.

You can get a sense for the ride quality of a motorhome without even driving it with a quick wheelbase calculation. The wheelbase is the horizontal distance between the centers of the front and rear wheels. In general, the longer the wheelbase, the better an RV will handle and the smoother the ride will be. To calculate, convert the RV length into inches and divide the wheelbase by the total length. The wheelbase should ideally be greater than 55 percent of the total length of the RV for better handling and ride quality on two-axle motorhomes. Tag axle motorhomes (with three axles) won't be impacted as much, as the third axle makes them more planted.

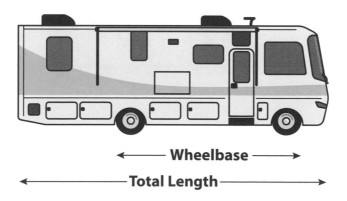

← Wheelbase →

← Total Length →

59   Use kitty litter for snow and ice traction.

While most RVers prefer to follow good weather, there are times you may find yourself stuck in snowy or icy conditions. Having some kitty litter on hand can help you get unstuck. Pour some on the snow and ice for substantially better traction.

60   Stay close to the center inside tunnels to maximize available height.

Tunnels usually have higher ceiling clearance in the center than the sides, so whenever height clearance is tight, drive as close as you can to the center of the road if necessary and possible (while staying in your lane, of course). If the tunnel offers more than one lane on your side of the road, choose the lane closest to the center on your side of the road.

61

Estimate your hitch/tongue weight.

As a general rule of thumb, the tongue/hitch weight capacity of your vehicle or RV is approximately 10 percent of the rated towing capacity. For example, if your vehicle is rated to tow 4,000 pounds, the tongue/hitch weight is likely to be around 400 pounds. Keep in mind that any cargo you are carrying inside the towing vehicle, especially in the rear of the vehicle, will reduce your available tongue/hitch weight capacity.

62   Review the campground route map before driving it.

Upon arrival at your campground, take the map you're given at check-in and review the route to your campsite before you leave the office. Some campground roads have tight turns, one-way streets, and even dead ends that can make it difficult to turn around. Review the campground map first to determine the most efficient route to your campsite and ensure you're coming up the correct way on the street so you can properly navigate your RV into your campsite.

63   Use cones for parking practice.

Practice maneuvering and backing large vehicles or trailers in an empty parking lot using safety cones. Build your skill and confidence in a safe, obstacle-free environment without an audience before hitting the road and having to deal with other vehicles, trees, and other hindrances.

64   Avoid parking near store entrances.

If you're parking your RV in a large parking lot, park as far from the entrance as you can. Choose your parking space wisely so that even if additional cars park nearby, you will still be able to exit with minimal hassle. The closer you park to the building, the more likely you are to get boxed in by another customer's vehicle.

65 Help your driver back up like a pro.

One of the best ways to guide a new, or even experienced, RVer in backing their trailer into a site is having the passenger stand next to the driver door, looking back toward the trailer. It allows close proximity communication and clear instructions.

HELEN STORR

"The simplest way we have found to back our trailer into a campsite is for me—the passenger—to get out of the vehicle and go around and stand beside my husband—the driver— with the window down. By standing facing the rear of the vehicle and trailer, I have maximum visibility. With his hands at '10 and 2' on the steering wheel, my husband starts backing the trailer. When I see the trailer needs to move to the right, I say 'right hand down' so he can pull the steering wheel down to the right, moving the trailer where it needs to go. If the trailer needs to move to the left, I say 'left hand down' and he pulls the steering wheel down to the left, adjusting the trailer direction as needed. This has been a great way for us to communicate clearly and in close proximity, without needing to raise our voices to hear each other while getting the trailer situated."

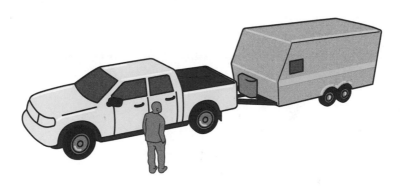

Slow down
to save
money.

66 **Keep your steering wheel cool when parked.**

When you park on hot days, use window shades and/or turn your steering wheel 180 degrees so the part of the wheel you hold to drive is shielded from the sun. When you start driving again, you won't burn your hands.

67 **Don't go into a parking lot if you don't know how to get out.**

Only enter a parking lot if you can also see the path to exit. The bigger the RV, the more this matters. For the sake of both safety and courtesy to other drivers, be sure the parking lot you're entering has an exit that will work for your RV.

68 **Buy a set of walkie-talkies for easy short-range communication.**

Bring a set of walkie-talkies along on your RV trips to use instead of cell phones to improve communication when navigating into your parking spots or if driving vehicles separately. This tip ensures good communication even in the spottiest of cell coverage areas.

69 **Book a pull-through campsite for easy entrance and exits.**

If you're driving a big rig or are otherwise uncomfortable backing your RV into your campsite, simply book a pull-through site at the campground. This will allow you to easily drive right in, then drive right out again. You may not even need to unhook your vehicle (if you are towing).

◄ *Mountain road in central Oregon / Photo © Julie Bennett*

70 **Use RV sign language when parking to make the process go smoothly.**

Develop and agree upon a good set of nonverbal hand and arm signals with your copilot as an additional form of communication while parking your RV at a campsite. Avoid shouting, causing a scene, and miscommunication by using large arm movements that are easily visible to the driver. For example, communicate "Stop" by lifting and crossing your arms in an X. Lift your arm up to shoulder height and bend at the elbow to motion forward, or motion to the side for moving left or right. Spread your arms apart and bring them closer to indicate remaining distance. You'll get your RV situated faster and without stress, and avoid a yelling match that could save your partnership and potential embarrassment!

BACK   STOP   LEFT

71 Back into your site from the driver's side.

The passenger side is known as the "blind side," so back your RV into a campsite from the driver side for maximum visibility. Plan your route within the campground accordingly to make sure you approach your site from the driver side whenever possible.

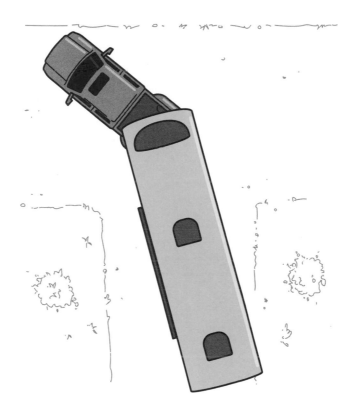

Chapter 2

REPAIRS AND MAINTENANCE

Your RV does have lots of unique parts and equipment. But don't let your fears about RV repairs, maintenance, or nasty sewer tank scenes turn you off RVing! In this chapter, you'll find a ton of handy hacks to keep you clean, safe, and well equipped to tackle RV jobs that can save you money and get you out of a bind when you're on the road.

Take time to discover
your personal travel style
and preferences.

72 **Book a service appointment right away.**

When you're buying a new RV, make an advance appointment for warranty repairs—with the dealer service center or manufacturer—before you even leave the dealership. Most new RVs have a "seasoning" period where they need adjustments and fixes. Allow enough time for you to take the RV out at least two to three times first to give it a "shakedown" and create a checklist of any items that need attention or repair. If you already have the appointment booked, you will be all set when you need it—and if by some chance, you don't, simply cancel. You can do this when buying a used RV too, but it's especially important when buying new, as new RVs almost always have bugs to be worked out, like a punch list on a newly built home.

73 **Protect your RV windshield wipers when parked.**

Get a piece of foam pipe insulation from the hardware store or slice through one side of a pool noodle. Slide the foam over your RV wiper blades whenever the RV is parked at a campsite or in storage. This will keep them free of debris like leaves, twigs, and dirt that may fall or blow onto your RV, and safeguard them from UV rays that can cause them to crack. Not only will this save you money since you won't have to replace expensive RV wiper blades as often, but it will also keep your windshield wipers clean and working more effectively when you use them.

74 **Avoid shocking your RV's electrical system.**

Use a separate external surge protector on your RV to avoid the potential for expensive damage to your rig. Some RV parks have outdated electrical systems, and it is not uncommon to see spikes or surges in power, especially on hot days with many campers running their air conditioners.

◀ *Padre Island National Seashore, Texas / Photo © Julie Bennett*

75   Create an RV routine maintenance schedule.

Review your RV owner's manual and all of the manuals that come with your RV systems and appliances to create a spreadsheet or calendar for maintaining and servicing each component of your RV, as recommended by the manufacturer. Or use an app or online tool like Maintain My RV to keep track.

DENNIS AND DONNA BARIL

"After reviewing the stack of manuals that came with our motorhome and knowing that many were available only online, I realized it would not be simple to put together an effective routine maintenance schedule. It would take time and experience. I decided to use an online program that would allow me to look at my RV maintenance history and make adjustments as additional information became known. Eventually, I had a list of practices that were simple to understand. I converted this to paper, and each month I can now perform all that is required and keep that month's sheet on file as a permanent record. After years of conducting routine maintenance, I can tell you this: We seem to have fewer surprises and generally lower-cost repairs with our rig than most other motorhome owners we meet along the way."

76   Divide and conquer tasks as a team.

Divide up the tasks for setting up and packing down your RV—on travel days and when you arrive at a campsite—among all of your passengers. When everyone has a list of specific responsibilities to follow, your group will increase efficiency and get the job done faster. This tip is great for team building and makes your RV camping trip a shared experience.

77   Get a grip.

Add strips of anti-slip grip tape to your RV entry steps to provide safer entry and exit for you and your pets. Prevent slipping in the shower by applying a few strips of grip tape on your bathroom shower floor.

78   Tilt your awning to prevent water pooling.

When your patio awning is out, keep it slightly tilted to one side or the other (so it's not perfectly straight) by extending one arm out slightly more than the other. Having one side angled slightly lower prevents water from pooling in the middle of the awning fabric and allows you to better control the direction water will run off when it rains.

79   Light up your RV entry.

Add reflective or glow-in-the-dark tape to your RV entry steps for better visibility at night. You could also install a battery-operated motion sensor light above your entry door.

80 Know your tires' age by the date code.

RV tires generally age out before they wear out because RVs usually don't travel as many miles as regular cars and trucks do. Generally, RV tires need replacing every 5–7 years, or less if they are worn or UV-damaged. The most important thing you can do for your RV safety is check your tires and replace them if they are aged out. Most tires have a four-digit code that will tell you when they were manufactured. Look for a four-digit number inside an oval circle on the tire sidewall. The first two digits represent the week of the year the tires were made, and the second two digits represent the year they were made. For example, 2921 would mean the tires were made in the twenty-ninth week of 2021.

81

Register your RV and appliances right away.

Unlike cars and trucks, your RV is assembled with all kinds of systems and appliances from several manufacturers—and all of them come with different warranties. So when you buy a new RV, make sure you register the vehicle itself with the RV manufacturer, then register the warranties for the other equipment with those manufacturers (e.g., refrigerator, microwave, water heater, stove, TVs, furnace, washer/dryer, fans, etc.). The process may take awhile, but when something goes wrong and needs fixing, it may be covered by the manufacturer's warranty for that particular component.

82   Carry a box of small spare parts and supplies.

To assemble a box, focus on the simple things you're willing and able to repair yourself. Walk through your critical RV systems—fuses, hydraulic fluid, brake fluid, light bulbs, plumber's tape, batteries, etc.—and keep a spare or two handy, along with the small tools you would need to make the repair yourself (e.g., a fuse puller, wrenches, screwdrivers).

TIM ROHRER OF OWNLESSDOMORE.US

"Our RV has hydraulic disc brakes, and I noticed the second brake hose had started leaking. I carry two spare hoses and the wrenches to replace it, so I made the repair and just 1 hour later, we were back on the road. Another common point of leaks is the water connections (because RV manufacturers use plastic), so I carry two straight and two elbow fittings, along with the necessary clamps. On Christmas Eve, I happened to notice our city water inlet was leaking. Thirty minutes later, without a trip to the hardware store, the line was fixed and the water back on."

83   Save your RV plumbing with a water pressure regulator.

Carry and use an adjustable water pressure regulator with a gauge to connect to the city water spigot. RV parks have water pressures that vary from as low as 15 to as high as 130 pounds per square inch (psi) of pressure. Many RV plumbing systems are meant to handle only 60 psi, and a burst pipe or water leak can cause serious and expensive damage to your RV. An adjustable water pressure regulator with a gauge allows you to measure and adjust to the pressure you want.

84 **Protect your RV tires from UV damage.**

RV tires can be very expensive to replace, and unfortunately, they usually age out before they wear out. UV rays from the sun over time cause silent damage to the tire sidewalls that can cause them to fail prematurely. So it's good practice to use light-colored tire covers when the RV will be sitting outside for a while. Applying a good UV inhibitor product to the sidewall also helps when the tire covers are not being used.

85 **Carry a 90-degree hose elbow to easily connect to water sources.**

Many campgrounds have a water faucet that is located very low to the ground, which makes it hard to attach a water hose to the faucet. Carry a small 90-degree metal elbow to attach to the faucet. Then you can more easily attach your hose to the other end of the elbow to the hose—nice and straight—without kinking. You can find these elbow attachments online and in most camping stores.

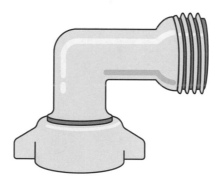

86   Warm your bays with light.

In subfreezing weather, place or hang an incandescent light bulb inside a shop light fixture in your RV wet bay and battery bay. This will keep those areas warm and help avoid freezing temperatures that can damage your equipment. You may be surprised at how much a simple light bulb can heat a small space. *But*, it must be incandescent, halogen, or other heat-producing light—don't use LEDs. When you're shopping for light bulbs, check the rating to see how much energy they use. The more energy a bulb uses, the more likely it will produce more heat. Make sure you stay at or under the maximum recommended wattage for the fixture.

87 **Protect your water systems in cold weather.**

When you're RVing in cold weather where the temperature may drop below freezing, fill your fresh water tank—at least halfway or completely—then disconnect your fresh water hose (and water filter, if you have one) from the faucet and store it inside. Then just use the water from your fresh tank until it's a safer temperature again outside.

DUANE LIPHAM OF RVINSPECTIONANDCARE.COM

"Extreme cold weather presents challenges for RVers. When the temperature drops to freezing or below, there is a chance that the water faucet and hose feeding water to your RV could freeze. If this goes on long enough, it could even freeze water inside your RV and burst your pipes. This danger was driven home for me in Texas, when we encountered a blast of cold weather that brought the nightly temperatures down to the mid-20s. I disconnected the water hose and emptied out all the water inside it, but I forgot to remove the water filter that was attached to the faucet. Next morning, I discovered the water filter was torn in half from the water inside the filter freezing and expanding in place. Now, anytime we're in very cold weather, I fill my fresh water tank first. Then I disconnect everything from the outside water faucet and run my water pump to provide water from the fresh water tank during the cold weather. Since we don't like to spend much time in very cold weather without moving, I don't usually need to do this for very long. But it helps ensure that I don't end up with any really expensive plumbing issues caused by extreme cold."

88 Install an inexpensive hitch ball cover.

Avoid messy grease stains and possible injuries by cutting open a tennis ball and using it to cover the hitch ball on your towing vehicle. The bright color of the tennis ball makes the hitch more visible, so you're less likely to bump into it, reducing the risk of both injuries and grease stains on your clothes.

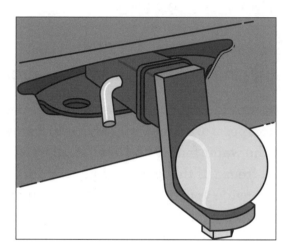

89 Level up before sliding out.

If your RV has slideouts, make sure your RV is fairly level before moving the slides in or out. This reduces strain on your slideout motors, makes them easier to operate, and reduces the risk of breaking your slideouts. Check with your manufacturer for specific leveling instructions for your RV as they can vary depending on your equipment.

90 Ask for help when you need it.

Got an RV problem you can't fix on your own? Don't worry; there are RV mechanics in most areas. Check your campground's visitor guide or ask the staff for a recommendation. Mobile RV mechanics will come to you, and they can fix most things on the "house" side of your RV (not the engine, however) fairly quickly.

91 Do the toilet paper test to be sure it's safe for your RV.

Find out if your favorite brand of toilet paper is septic safe—and therefore suitable for use in an RV—by placing a sheet of TP in a jar or container of water. Seal it with a lid and let it sit for about 5 minutes. Give the container or jar a good shake—if the TP sheet stays intact, you cannot safely use that TP in your RV plumbing system. If the TP sheet easily breaks up into many little pieces, it is septic safe and therefore okay to use in your RV toilet. Reminder: Don't flush anything down an RV toilet except what comes out of your body and septic-safe TP.

Eight Tips for Avoiding a Sewer Disaster!

92 Avoid the pyramid of poo.

Keep the black tank valve closed until you're ready to dump your tanks so your number twos don't dry up, pile up, and harden, making it very difficult to remove them. Wait until waste tanks are at least half full before dumping so you have plenty of liquid to wash everything away.

93 Empty the black tank first.

Then open the gray tank valve to flush out and clean the sewer hose of any remaining black tank contents. It's safe to leave your gray tank valve open—just make sure you close it for a day or two before emptying the black tank so you have enough water to flush out the hose and avoid a stinky slinky.

94 Don't cheap out on your hose.

Spend the extra bucks on a decent-quality sewer hose—it's the last thing you want to fail when dumping your black tank!

95 Offer support.

Use a sewer hose support to keep your sewer hose off the ground (mandatory in some counties). This creates a better angle for water flow, and it prevents the hose from snaking around wildly like a garden hose and creating a real mess for you and your neighbors.

96 Treat your system.

Use an RV-friendly toilet tank treatment product like Happy Campers to break down solids and neutralize tank smells.

97 Stay sanitary.

Keep disinfecting wipes and disposable gloves handy in your RV wet bay area to stay clean and avoid contamination when doing dirty jobs.

98 Secure your connection.

Make sure you screw the sewer hose attachment securely to the dump outlet. Keep it in place at the end with your foot, a stone, or other heavy object to prevent it from coming loose and spewing your sewage.

99 Flush the tank.

If your RV has a black tank rinse/flush feature, use it often after dumping to keep your black tank nice and clean (well, relatively speaking). If you camp often, aim to flush and rinse the black tank every other time you dump, when hooked up at a full hookup campsite. If you only camp occasionally, flush and rinse your tank before you put your RV back into storage.

100 Store your RV awning when away to protect it from wind damage.

One of the most common things to break on an RV is the awning. This can be both expensive and a nuisance to repair or replace. Keep an eye on weather forecasts for windy weather so you know when to bring the awning in. And if you're going to be away from the RV for a while, stow the awning away while you're gone. Winds can kick up quickly—often without any warning or forecasts—and it's better to be safe than sorry.

101 Protect your slideout seals.

Take care of your rubber slideout seals by applying a UV protectant like 303 Aerospace Protectant. This helps to prevent them from drying out and keeps a better seal.

102 Take off dirty gloves right away.

You may remember to put on protective gloves for doing dirty jobs like dumping your sewer tank, but it can be easy to forget to remove them right away. Don't go touching anything else while wearing the gloves—like the water faucet, door handle, keys, and so on—to avoid cross contamination of nasty germs.

103 Remove dead bugs with dryer sheets.

Use damp dryer sheets to clean dead bugs and insects from the front of your RV, truck, and windshield after a drive. They won't hurt your paint but are very effective for getting bugs off, especially if you clean those bug guts as soon as possible.

▶ *Mountain road in western Colorado / Photo © Julie Bennett*

Tint your RV windows
to keep it cool.

104   Use noodles to protect your noggin.

Cut lengths of pool noodles or pipe insulators and place them along the edges of your slideouts when they are extended. You will be glad you did—especially if the slideouts are above storage bays—as you'll be less likely to bump your head when accessing them. Pool noodles are bigger and thicker and come in bright colors for better visibility, while gray-black pipe insulators are more discreet if you prefer that style. Both are inexpensive. Pool noodles are also useful as protection on awning support arms, stakes in the ground, and much more. Just remember to remove them before bringing your slideouts back in so that they don't get in the way of the slide fully closing.

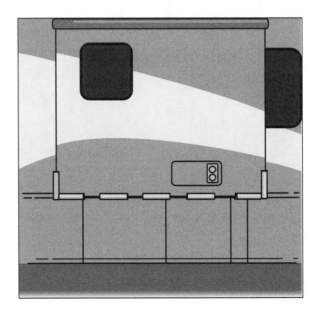

105   Clean your tanks for accurate gauge readings.

If your wastewater tank level gauges are not reading correctly, fill your black or gray tanks ¼–½ full with hot, soapy water before your next drive to slosh it around and clean the gunk off the walls of the tank and sensors. You can also pour a bag or two of ice cubes down the toilet (instead of hot water) to help knock off stubborn gunk stuck on the walls of your black tank where the sensors are located. By the time you arrive at your destination, the ice should be melted and ready to dump. Take your "drive and clean routine" up a notch by adding a cup of Calgon bath beads to help soften the water and/or a bottle of Pine-Sol if you want to clean the tank and reduce odors. Then dump and rinse your tanks when you arrive at your destination.

106   Deter RV pests with everyday items.

When you're storing your RV, Irish Spring soap bars and steel wool can both be effective deterrents for rodents and pests. Place soap shavings around the tires or any area of the RV that touches the ground. You can also put soap in areas that are especially attractive to pests, like the back side of your propane RV fridge. It will deter them and keep your RV smelling fresh. Additional tips include putting a flea collar on the floor behind the RV fridge area and placing steel wool in areas with gaps, such as where a water or sewer hose goes through a hole, to fill gaps and keep rodents at bay.

107

Coil and connect your hoses.

When you're getting ready to leave your campsite and packing everything away, drain the fluids from both fresh water and sewer hoses. Then coil them up and connect the hose ends to each other. This keeps your hoses tidier and better organized, reduces leaks and spillage on travel days, and increases sanitation.

108 Do quick measurements before putting out slides.

Before setting up your campsite and extending slideouts, do this quick DIY measurement to ensure slides won't hit obstacles—no tape measure required! Measure the depth of your RV slide-out(s) while the slide is extended by standing next to the slide-out with your back against the wall of the RV. Extend your arm out 90 degrees and note where the slideout ends compared to your arm. Whenever you're parking in a tight campsite and worried about hitting a tree or other obstacle with your slide-out, put your mind at ease by simply standing with your back against the RV and putting your arm out. You'll immediately know if it will fit before setting your RV up in your campsite. Use the same technique for all slideouts and storage bays to ensure you don't park too close to obstacles that may cause damage or limit access.

109   Freeze a coin to confirm food safety.

Don't flip a coin to determine if your food is safe; *freeze* a coin and be sure. If you plan to leave your RV unattended or in storage with the fridge running, fill a container halfway with water, seal with a lid, then freeze it. When it's fully frozen, open the lid, place a coin on top of the ice, reseal, and place the container back in the freezer. If your RV fridge loses power long enough to allow the water to melt, the coin will drop down below the surface, showing how deep the thaw was, even if power comes back on and the water refreezes. If you return to find the coin still on top of the ice, you'll know the temperature stayed consistent. If the coin is at the bottom, you should probably discard everything in the fridge and freezer, as you'll know the temperature dropped for long enough to make the food unsafe to consume.

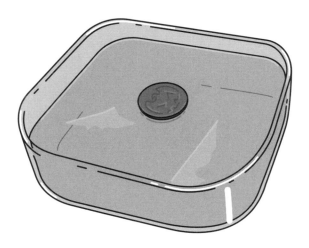

110 Save money on RV antifreeze.

When winterizing your RV, instead of filling your fresh water tank with antifreeze (use the kind specifically designed for RV water systems), get an extra piece of water line to connect to your water pump intake side. Use this alternate hose to dip into jugs of RV antifreeze when winterizing to reduce the amount of RV antifreeze needed by going directly into the plumbing instead of through the fresh water tank.

Water Pump

111 Clean your awning the simple way.

Extend your awning and coat it with an RV awning cleaner, then roll the awning back up. Let it sit for 15 minutes while the cleaner soaks into the fabric, then unroll your awning and rinse it off.

112 Tint your RV windows to keep it cool.

Apply window tint film to your RV skylight and windows to reduce solar heat gain and UV rays while increasing privacy inside your RV.

113 Make quick and strong repairs with EternaBond tape.

Keep a roll of EternaBond seam and leak repair tape handy to repair roof leaks, seal seams, fix tears, patch hoses, or make minor repairs to torn awnings, tents, kayaks, and camping chairs. Just don't put this tape on anything for a temporary fix with plans to remove it. It is called EternaBond for a reason and can last for well over 20 years.

114 Dehumidify for faster drying and prevent mold.

In humid climates, the condensation from showering, cooking, and even just breathing in an RV can make the air feel clammy, cause mold, and prevent towels from drying. If you have a built-in air conditioner or heat pump, you can run one of those to dehumidify the RV. Or use a stand-alone dehumidifier in humid climates to help keep the air drier and help towels dry faster without warming or cooling the RV.

115 Carry lightweight mats for working on the RV.

Carry a couple of interlocking foam gym mats—or a small yoga mat—to use when kneeling or lying down to work on your RV. This will keep you off the ground while providing a cushion to keep you more comfortable.

116 Support your entry steps for safe entrances and exits.

Place leveling blocks or a small jack (bottle jacks are compact) under your RV entry steps to make them feel sturdier and less wobbly.

117   Check your RV propane level without a gauge.

Fill a gallon-sized pitcher, a pot, or a small pail with hot tap water. (Boiling water isn't needed, and about a gallon is plenty.) Pour the entire pitcher of water down one side of the propane tank, wetting the exterior from top to bottom. Then place the palm of your hand on the wet area of the tank. The hot water makes the metal warm to the touch. But due to the extremely cold temperature of propane, the lower part of the tank will be cold. Move your hand up or down until you feel where the warm (upper) part of the tank meets the cold (lower) part of the tank. That dividing line will reveal the exact level of the propane in the tank.

PETER KNIZE AND JOHN SULLIVAN OF THERVGEEKS.COM AND HOSTS OF THE RVERS TV SHOW

"We've all been there. You go outside to flip the food on the grill, and it's cold—both the food and the grill! While our large motorhome has a built-in propane tank with a gauge, we used to wonder about the accuracy of the reading. Even if gauges are consistent, they can be consistently wrong. Using this hot water trick allowed us to know exactly what ½ or ¼ tank equates to on our rig. RVers with portable propane tanks can pick them up to get an approximation of how much propane is remaining based on weight. But that requires removing and lifting the tanks. Larger ones can be quite heavy, so removing any hold-down straps, then picking them up, to get only an approximate volume level can be a nuisance. Pouring hot water down the side of the tank doesn't require removing it from the RV, or lifting it. Best of all, it allows for a much more accurate reading of propane level. And in cold weather, the warm water and metal of the tank also feel good on your hand!"

118 Don't be shocked by your power pedestal.

Always turn the power *off* at the power pedestal breaker before plugging in—or unplugging—your RV to avoid a potential shock to you or the RV.

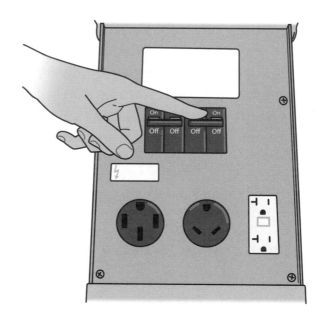

119 Unclog blocked drains with this septic-safe solution.

Sinks not draining properly? First, remove the metal sink drain cover and use a plastic drain snake to remove any clumps of hair, then run some hot water. Next, pack the drain with a cup of baking soda, then pour half a cup of white vinegar into the drain. It will cause a reaction and start bubbling up quite a bit. You could also mix the baking soda and vinegar in a container, stir, and quickly pour the mixture down the drain. Leave it for 30–60 minutes to break up the clogged gunk. Follow up by pouring a gallon or two of hot water down the drain to flush away your troubles for a cheap and easy septic-safe drain fix.

120 **Block solar rays from the outside.**

Use external window shades on your RV's windshield to reduce the solar heat gain streaming into your RV. Being able to block the sun's rays before they even get inside your RV makes a huge difference compared to simply having inside window shades or coverings.

121 **Move your manual stabilizer jacks with ease.**

Use a cordless power drill and a socket attachment to quickly and easily raise and lower your trailer stabilizer jacks instead of winding them manually with a hand crank. The drill method is much faster and easier. (But keep the original hand crank on board in case the socket breaks or your drill battery dies.)

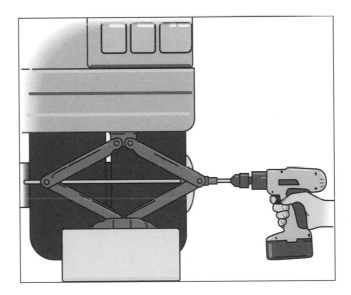

122   Save on labor by replacing cheap parts sooner.

If your RV is in the shop for a repair with a substantial amount of labor involved, ask the repair technician if there are any other inexpensive parts in that area of the equipment that could also be replaced as a preventive measure. This idea can help avoid a future costly repair for a cheap part that's hard to get to.

123   Fix a leaky toilet with vinegar.

Unlike plumbing in a traditional house, many RV toilets keep water in the bowl using a rubber gasket. Sometimes this seal can start to leak if there is a buildup of lime or other deposits. If your toilet bowl is not holding water well, first try pouring some white vinegar in the bowl and letting it sit for 30 minutes or longer. This should dissolve the deposits and resolve the issue. If not, you might need to scrape the gasket with a plastic knife or spoon. Then apply some plumbers' grease to give the gasket an even better seal.

124   Wax on to keep bugs off.

Removing bug guts from the front of your RV is just one part of the fun of RVing during warmer months. Before hitting the road for a long haul, clean and wax the front of your RV. Doing so will help bug guts wipe off much easier later on with a wet rag or gas station squeegee.

125

Track generator hours to weigh solar benefits.

When camping off-grid, track your generator usage by logging the number of hours used to estimate what you spend on generator fuel. If you're ever considering a power upgrade, you can quickly estimate how soon an investment in solar panels and/or lithium batteries would become financially worthwhile.

126 **Keep insects out of exhaust vents.**

Both the RV furnace and water heater have exhaust vents that port to the outside of the RV. Unfortunately, those vents are large enough for insects (or other critters) to enter and make a home or nest inside. This can cause poor performance for the furnace or water heater or even foul it up enough to require a repair. Get some mesh vent screens and install them over the exterior vents. The screens still allow a free flow of air from the appliance to the outside while preventing insects, rodents, or bats from getting inside into the vent area. You can find these screens online and in most camping stores.

127 **Reclaim items that fall under or behind your slides.**

If something in your RV falls onto the floor and rolls under your slideout, try to reach it with an unwound and bent wire coat hanger. Or go outside and move the slide seal to access it from the back side.

128   Store your RV cover in a garbage can.

Those large RV covers used to protect your RV during winter months are awkward to handle and difficult to store when they're not being used. Once removed from its storage bag, the storage cover is almost impossible to get back in! Toss the original bag and simply get a large rolling garbage can. You can easily stuff the RV cover in there, along with everything that comes with it. Then roll it away until you need it again.

129   Label each tire's proper pressure.

Knowing your proper tire inflation pressure is key to safe driving and better gas mileage. With multiaxle rigs and tow cars, you may find yourself with three or four different tire pressure psi numbers to remember based on axle location. Pick up a DYMO or similar type of label maker and create a label for each axle's correct psi and place the label on the fender's edge above each tire. You won't be able to see the stickers when normally looking at your RV, but when you bend down to fill your tires, look up and there it will be, reminding you of correct pressure at each axle.

130   Don't rush into RV upgrades.

Avoid making major upgrades to your RV during the first year. You may be tempted to start upgrading or adding cool new equipment like a new refrigerator, solar panels, or a large battery bank to your new RV. Take time to discover your personal travel style and preferences first. Really get to know your RV's features and limitations before you make those decisions. The valuable information gathered in these first outings will clearly define what your needs are. You can then spend your money wisely on upgrades that will really benefit you and your style of RVing.

BRIAN PURSEL OF RVWITHTITO.COM

"For many years traveling with our kids we primarily visited RV parks and full-hookup campgrounds. The stock capabilities of our Class C motorhome got us through long travel days and a night or two on generator power. When we realized that just one house battery wasn't cutting it, I upgraded to two. Everything changed once our kids grew up and moved away. We became much more spontaneous in our traveling style and preferred camping in remote areas. We made one or two upgrades each year based on what we felt was lacking. As we used those new features, we would assess what worked well and what our limitations were. That has helped us prioritize the upgrades for the next year. Eventually we reached the point where we could be completely self-sufficient and use our RV the way we wanted to, camping almost exclusively off the grid."

131 Light up the night and free up your hands.

An LED headlight is a very helpful tool to keep in your RV. Having your hands free for repairs while also having the light point in the direction you are looking can mean the difference between a simple fix and needing a second pair of hands (which might not be available). Pick a headlamp that is rechargeable, ensuring you won't be burning through batteries. What's better, some models use your phone charger so you can keep your cord count to a minimum.

Chapter 3

CAMPING, CAMP-GROUNDS, AND BOONDOCKING

Whether you like to camp in RV parks, at RV rally events, or off the grid, here are some proven hacks that will help you make the most of your stay. Discover tips for finding great campsites (even in a big rig), ways to save time and money, and methods for boondocking like a pro.

Discover hidden gems.

132 Use top apps and websites for finding where to stay.

The following websites and apps are the best suited for RV travelers: AllStays, *Big Rigs Best Bets*, *Boondockers Welcome*, Boondocking.org, Campendium, CampgroundReviews.com, CampgroundViews.com, FreeRoam, Harvest Hosts, Hipcamp, KOA, Recreation.gov, ReserveAmerica, RV LIFE, RVontheGo .com, RV Parks & Campgrounds, The Dyrt, Togo RV, Tripadvisor, Ultimate Canada Public Campgrounds, Ultimate US Public Campgrounds, US Public Lands.

133 Arrive near checkout time for best site availability.

If you're trying to get into a campground that does not accept reservations, you will find the best (most) availability of campsites is right around or shortly after the official checkout time.

134 Pick up last-minute reservations.

You can try to score a last-minute RV camping reservation at booked campgrounds by calling the RV park a couple of days before you plan to arrive—or even on the same day—as that is when most people cancel their reservations. Have a list of four or five potential campgrounds scoped out in advance, ordered by preference, to try to nab a spot.

135 Check online campground maps before booking.

Before making reservations, check the campground website to view the site map and amenities. You may be able to request a specific site or at least ask to be near certain features you want. For example, if you have kids, a site near the playground might be convenient so you can easily keep an eye on them. If you prefer to use campground facilities instead of the bathroom in your RV, ask for a campsite situated near a bathhouse.

◀ *Henrys Lake State Park, Island Park, Idaho / Photo © Julie Bennett*

136 Expand your campground search radius.

Most campers make the mistake of thinking they need to stay right in the middle of it all to have the best experience. The advantage of camping is having the flexibility to expand your search to find amazing places. For example, if you want to camp on the floor of Yosemite National Park, the choices are very limited (four campgrounds). But if you search a 50-mile radius around Yosemite, you'll find over one hundred potential campgrounds. Some of them are as amazing, if not more amazing, than the valley floor locations, and they will often be less crowded and less expensive.

137 Discover hidden gems.

Instead of relying on local tourism guides, ask the locals for their personal favorites and recommendations when visiting an area. You may discover lesser-known hidden gems while avoiding the crowds and having a unique experience.

138 Make reservations for certain busy dates.

You definitely need reservations for special dates and times where flexibility is limited. Want to stay at a specific campground? Book in advance. Planning a big-get together with friends and family? Book well in advance. When you absolutely need or want to be in a certain spot on a certain date, advance bookings are critical.

139 Ask the locals for cheap RV parking.

If you're looking for a place to stay with your RV, post an ad on the local *Craigslist* or *Facebook Marketplace*. You might find some inexpensive and unique opportunities to park on locals' land, or even trade your services to earn a few bucks by working at a farm, helping with a project, or even just keeping an eye on property for somebody.

140 Save a bundle with camping memberships.

Some campground networks offer memberships that can save you a fair bit of money if you camp regularly. Memberships with Thousand Trails, Coast to Coast, Passport America, KOA, Good Sam, and others can save you hundreds, or even thousands, of dollars per year. For an annual fee, some programs give you access to free camping at various unusual locations. For example, through Harvest Hosts you can stay at wineries, farms, golf courses, and other attractions, while *Boondockers Welcome* allows you to stay on private host properties.

JULIE BENNETT OF RVLOVE.COM AND COAUTHOR OF *LIVING THE RV LIFE* AND *RV HACKS*

"One of the ways we were able to afford full-time RVing was by carefully planning our budget! We realized early on that campground fees would likely be one of our biggest expenses. So we looked into the different kinds of camping memberships available to see which ones would more than pay for themselves and help bring our average nightly cost down. By far, the biggest savings for us came from our investment in a Thousand Trails camping membership. We started with the basic annual camping pass but eventually upgraded to a membership with even more benefits. This brought our nightly camping fees down to under $9 a night. Do your homework to decide which memberships work best for you. We wrote several in-depth articles and expense reports at our blog to help others learn how they can find different ways to save money on RV camping too. RVing is a great lifestyle, but it's even better when you can make it more affordable!"

141 Check event calendars first.

When making your travel plans, check for major holidays as well as local events in the area at the time you plan to visit before making your reservation. For example, if you're an avid motorcyclist, you may like to tie your visit to the Black Hills of South Dakota in with the annual Sturgis Motorcycle Rally in August, an event that attracts hundreds of thousands of people to the area. But if you prefer to explore Mount Rushmore and Custer State Park when it's not so busy, you'll want to avoid major holiday weekends and big events like Sturgis that draw large crowds and inflate nightly campground rates. Some RV parks will book up months or even years in advance for special events like music festivals or a total solar eclipse, so plan your route to coincide either with them or to avoid them, depending on your preference.

142 Stay midweek for smaller crowds and lower prices.

You will often find RV parks have higher availability and lower prices on weekdays, so if you have a flexible schedule, plan on staying Sunday through Thursday instead of over the weekend. The RV park will be less crowded and may save you a few bucks too.

143 Visit tourist hotspots at shoulder seasons or in the off-season.

Popular tourist spots are always crowded at peak times, so if you can schedule your visit for off-peak and shoulder seasons, you will experience smaller crowds and sometimes better prices. Visiting locations at the beginning of a tourist season can also be better than mid- or late season, as the locals are more rested and welcoming of tourists than they are later in the tourist season when they're tired and ready for a break.

144

Maximize points with a travel-friendly credit card.

Travel hack your way to even more free travel by using credit cards and loyalty programs that will maximize your points accumulated for spending on travel and accommodation. The most common expenses for RVers are campgrounds, fuel, and restaurants—and you can earn two or three points for every dollar you spend in these categories, so look for cards that can earn you free travel (or bonus credit) faster.

145 Save money with longer stays.

Many RV parks offer weekly rates that average out to a cheaper nightly fee—a deal like "pay for six nights, get the seventh night free" is common. Save even more with monthly (or even seasonal/quarterly) stays, which can save you a bundle if you spend extended time in your RV. A slower travel pace will also save on fuel. Plus, staying longer allows you to immerse more in an area for a more fulfilling experience as a local instead of as a tourist.

146 Get a national park pass for cheap or free.

Access more than two thousand federal recreation sites—like national parks, wildlife refuges, or spots owned by the US Forest Service or US Army Corps of Engineers—with an America the Beautiful Pass, for free or on the cheap. Regular passes are $80 annually, but you may qualify for a discounted or even free pass if you are over 62 years old, in the military (or are a veteran or Gold Star Family), are someone with a permanent disability, or a fourth grader. Visit www.nps.gov to see all pass savings options.

147 Be creative when parking to get better views.

If it isn't against the campground rules—and you won't annoy your neighbors by going awning-to-awning—consider getting creative in how you park your RV in your designated campsite. Backing in, pulling in forward, or even pulling in diagonally can help you get better views from your windows. If you spend a lot of time at home in your RV working, optimizing your office view could end up being one of your most important steps in setting up camp!

148 Use a rope to mark out a parking spot.

When you are parking in a tight spot, traveling solo, or otherwise needing to have a very accurate visual marker to know where to situate your RV, use a rope to create a precise outline of where you want the RV to end up.

KEN STORR

"Here's a handy rope trick I use for doing a perfect park in my RV, even when I don't have a copilot to help navigate. Cut a piece of a rope that is equivalent to the length of the RV plus double the RV width. Measure in the width of your RV at both ends of the rope and mark the spots with a permanent marker or wrap the rope with a piece of colored tape. This creates a clearly marked three-sided outline of your RV. Before pulling into your campsite, lay the rope in a U shape outlining the position where you want to park your RV. Use the rope as your guideline when backing in to nail the perfect park every time!"

149 Park to create your optimal temperature environment.

Park your RV deliberately to take advantage of your preferred conditions at any time of the year. For early morning sun, park with your windows facing east. For a sunny patio, position your RV so the patio is facing the south side. For a more shaded patio, park so it's facing west.

150 Use natural fencing for protection.

When boondocking, instead of parking out in the wide-open spaces, park near natural features like creeks, trees, bushes, or other natural boundaries to help create a more homey and protected campsite feel. You will feel more nestled in, and it can offer more privacy and separation if other campers come to the area.

151 Clean the water spigot before hooking up.

Before you connect your fresh drinking water hose, wipe the campground water spigot down first with a Lysol or Clorox disinfecting wipe. Or at the very least, turn on the faucet and run some water through it before connecting your hose to reduce contamination from the previous site occupant. You never know what the previous occupant did last.

▶ *Medina Lake RV Campground, Lakehills, Texas / Photo © Julie Bennett*

Save a bundle with
camping memberships.

152   Know where you are in case of emergency.

When traveling, you may not immediately remember where you are, especially when just waking up or dealing with a stressful or emergency situation. As soon as you arrive at an RV park, keep the campground welcome brochure with its contact information in a consistent, prominent location in your RV so you'll know where it is at all times—on the fridge, by the bed, at the entry, or on the dashboard. In case of emergency, you can quickly share your location and address with emergency responders. You could also use your phone to take a snapshot of the campground brochure's contact info and text it to a family member or close friend. It can be reassuring for family and friends to know where you are, plus they will know whom to contact in case of an emergency.

153   Break up long drives with free overnight stays.

In many towns, some big stores like Walmart, Cracker Barrel, Cabela's, and Bass Pro Shops—and even some shopping centers and casinos—allow free RV overnight stays in their parking lots. But not all locations or city ordinances allow it, so always call ahead or check with the manager or security to get permission first; otherwise, you may get ticketed or asked to move in the middle of the night. Remember, these aren't campgrounds, so respect their property and requirements. Park as far away from the entrance as possible. Don't set up camp—that means no camp chairs, barbecues, or awnings out. Keep your slideouts in if at all possible. Don't put your leveling jacks down, as they can damage the asphalt surface. And say thank you by supporting their business with a purchase. Some restaurants and bars in smaller towns may even allow you to stay overnight in their parking lots if you eat or drink there.

154

Watch movies under the stars.

Head outside for movie night with family or friends. Hang a white sheet on the side of your RV as an outdoor projector screen and use a mini-projector and speakers to show a movie or share photos on a big screen. Just be mindful you're not bothering your camping neighbors if you're staying in a campground.

155 **Find your RV via your phone's map while in unfamiliar places.**

When you arrive at a boondocking site, use Google Maps to pin your location so you can share it with others and also find your location more easily in the dark using GPS. Remote campsites can be difficult to find in the dark, even if you're not far away.

156 **Deter bugs with campfire smoke.**

A bit of smoke from a campfire on your clothes is a good bug deterrent, and will have your clothes and RV smelling like campfire the next day (which some folks really like).

157 **Create a community atmosphere.**

When traveling with friends and camping off-grid together, you might want to park in a circle to create a central gathering area. With all patios facing each other, this arrangement creates a mini-community and an easy way to share the campsite area. As the day turns to night, the changing position of sun and shade can naturally shift the gathering spaces from one RV to another.

158 **Use water jugs as weights.**

Carry empty plastic milk jugs (with a handle) and fill them with water when you get to your campsite and use them as weights on windy days. For example, you could place them on your camping mat, secure them with a rope to your TV dish, or secure them to your awning arms/stakes. You can even use these water-filled jugs for a light-duty weight-lifting workout.

159 **Secure cabinets with bungee cords, hair ties, or rubber bands.**

Use bungee cords, hair ties, or strong rubber bands on the handles and knobs of cabinets to keep them closed during travel. This is especially important if you have any cabinets that are behind slideouts when closed. Even if the contents temporarily push open the cabinet, the rubber band or bungee cord should close it back up. If cabinets behind a slideout open during travel, they may jam up or tear the cabinet door right off its bracket when you try to extend the slideout. We found some great strong rubber bands in Maine for this purpose, where they use them to secure lobster claws!

160

Pack up the night before.

If you need to leave a campground early in the morning, do most of your packing up the night before. It is faster and less likely to disrupt neighbors, especially if you're departing during "quiet hours." You'll also want to do this if bad weather is in the forecast—nobody likes packing things up in the wind or rain.

161 Keep firewood local.

If you plan on burning a wood fire, use only local wood that you purchase nearby. Transporting wood from outside the area can accidentally introduce harmful insects or tree diseases.

162 Avoid a spider scare.

Some campsites have the water hookup below ground, requiring you to reach into a hole to access the water connection. Before you reach in, put on some gloves if desired and swirl a stick around the hole to clean up spiderwebs and make sure no unexpected creatures are down there.

163 Light your fire with your snacks.

Use a handful of corn chips wrapped in a paper towel as a starter for your campfire.

Ten Ways to Conserve Water Off the Grid

164 Take a Navy shower.

Get wet, turn off water to lather up, rinse off, done.

165 Capture cold shower water.

Don't let the water go down the drain while waiting for it to warm up. Capture in a bucket or pitcher and reuse in the kitchen or to flush the toilet.

166 Turn on a trickle.

Don't turn water on full blast—a trickle is usually enough for brushing teeth and washing hands.

167 Wipe down your dishes.

Use paper towels to wipe down dishes to preclean them so you need less water for dishwashing.

168 Wash dishes once a day.

Let precleaned dishes sit, and wash only once per day.

169 Reuse your dishwater.

After doing dishes, save the water to flush your toilet.

170 Prewash your produce.

Before your trip, prewash all fruit and veggies.

171 Pre-prepare meals.

Precooked meals will save time and use fewer dishes in prep when reheating, especially foods with high water use, like pasta and rice.

172 Use paper plates.

Avoid dishwashing altogether, and reuse your dirty plates to start your campfire.

173 Swap showers for body wipes.

Skip showers or have them less often, and just freshen up and wipe away grime with wet body wipes.

174 **Show you're not home alone.**

If you are a solo traveler or concerned about your safety, buy a used pair of large men's boots or shoes from a thrift store and leave them outside your RV. You can do the same with large dog bowls, or put two camping chairs out at your campsite. These will send the message that you aren't home alone and can increase your peace of mind as well as your safety.

175 **Create a portable outdoor paper towel holder.**

Use a metal garden flag stand as a handy, portable paper towel holder for outside use. Simply insert into the ground near your barbecue, picnic table, or where you're doing mechanical or other dirty jobs around the RV so you'll always have easy access to wipe things up.

176   Enjoy campfires safely year-round.

If you're staying in places that often have fire bans, use a portable propane firepit instead of a traditional wood campfire. (Propane firepits are usually allowed even during fire restrictions.) You can even use the same propane tank with a barbecue. Propane firepits start and extinguish quickly and safely, don't give off smoke that can get in your eyes or bother allergy sufferers, and offer a flame that is more predictable, so unexpected sparks won't fly out to scare or injure people or pets. You can also use the campfire in your backyard at home for warmth and ambience when you're not out camping.

177   Use nonlethal tools for protection.

Increase your personal safety by carrying a can of bear spray or a dual-purpose flashlight with built-in PepperBall launcher. Keep in a handy place near the entry door of your RV by day, and by the bed at night as a strong, nonlethal deterrent for threats—whether four-legged or human. Unlike firearms and other weapons, bear spray is legal for its intended use in all fifty US states and across Canada. PepperBall launchers are generally acceptable in more states than firearms, but you still need to check state laws for their use.

178 Keep your wheels on the ground to minimize suspension strain.

If your motorized RV has trouble leveling on a sloped RV site, use leveling blocks to even things out and keep your tires firmly planted. While leveling jacks are helpful, you don't want to rely on them solely if it means they lift your tires off the ground like your RV is about to take off! That is less stable, and also puts your RV's leveling system and suspension under unnecessary strain. If you still can't get level, consider parking your RV in the opposite direction in your campsite—even if it means you need to run the water hose and/or power cord underneath the RV to reach hookups on the other side.

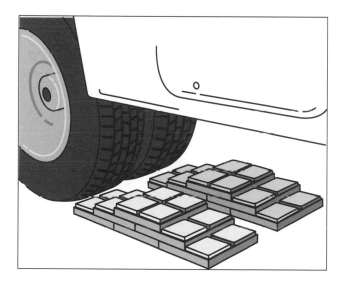

179

Dehumidify your RV with the air conditioner or heat pump.

Running the RV's air conditioner or electric heat pump will help dehumidify the inside of your RV. (Running the propane furnace adds humidity in addition to heat.) So when conditions allow it, use the electric heat pump to stay warm on cool nights instead of running the furnace. However, electric heat pumps don't usually work very well below 35°F, so if you do need to run your propane furnace, crack a window open for reduced humidity.

180 Be wary if you carry a firearm.

If you plan on carrying a firearm, make sure you check the laws where you plan to travel through and to. Laws vary across the fifty US states, and even if you have a permit to carry in your home state, it may still be illegal to possess these weapons in other states. Check what's legal and what's not before you travel to, or through, states at websites like GunLawsbyState .com. Firearms are more highly restricted in Canada and are illegal to carry into Mexico, so do your homework well in advance before crossing any international borders. Check the US Customs and Border Protection website, plus each country's website for the latest restrictions or requirements before you travel there.

181 Improve your security.

Hiding valuables in a stealthy place is better security than simply locking them away in the RV. The entry and storage bay locks are often of poor quality and not nearly as good as home locks. In fact, many RVs even use the same key, so install an aftermarket key lock or even a keyless door lock so you can enter a code you set yourself.

182 Protect wood cabinets from drying out.

If you're storing your RV in a hot, dry environment in between camping trips, keep a bucket of water in your RV to protect the wood from drying out. The water helps moderate the temperature while adding humidity to the RV interior. Keep the bucket inside the shower or in the kitchen sink to avoid splashing onto floors in case you forget about it when you next move the RV.

183   Create a DIY outdoor handwashing station.

Save on water and trips in and out of the RV by creating your own outside handwashing station. Thoroughly clean out a laundry detergent or plastic beverage dispenser, then fill it with soapy water. Keep it outside on a table with a roll of paper towels on a stand, a hand sanitizer pump dispenser, and hand wipes too. It's a great way to keep kids outside and keep hands (and the RV) clean(er) without everyone needing to traipse in and out to use up water from your fresh tanks, especially if you're out boondocking.

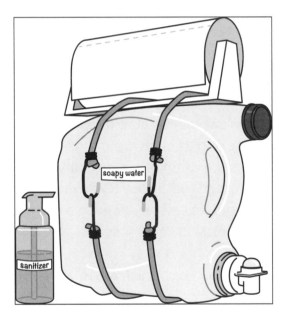

184 Be prepared to act fast in extreme weather.

When traveling in tornado or hurricane season, keep a go bag ready with medications, a cell phone charger, and important documents. Keep warm clothes and a rain poncho easily accessible so you can head to a concrete or other safe building, like a bathroom block, or leave the area to stay at a nearby home of a family or friend. If you have a smartphone, it will often alert you to severe weather in the area. Install apps like NOAA Weather Radar Live or Weather High-Def Radar with alerts, or carry a weather radio to stay informed of approaching storms.

185 Prevent mold and mildew when in humid places.

Keep dehumidifying products (like DampRid) inside your RV when traveling or storing your RV in humid climates to prevent mold and mildew. Wipe out an empty fridge and leave the door ajar and keep cabinet doors open for more air circulation. Water and mold are two of the most common causes of RV damage.

186 Leave cabinet doors open in extreme weather.

If it's very cold or very hot outside, leave your RV cabinet doors open to help keep the contents at a more moderate temperature, especially if you store temperature-sensitive items inside.

187 Insulate your ceiling vents.

To significantly reduce heat loss on cold nights or help reduce heat gain on hot days, stuff pillows or RV vent cushions into your ceiling vents.

Maximize your
solar power.

188   Use Bubble Wrap for insulation.

Using foil Bubble Wrap in your RV cabinets and windows is an effective insulator, but the foil blocks out all the light too. Use clear Bubble Wrap on windows for increased insulation without blocking the light.

189   Bring in your slides in chilly weather.

If you're RVing in very cold weather, consider bringing in one or more of your slideouts. This will result in a smaller area to heat, and the RV will be more tightly sealed. With less air space, and less exposed wall space, the RV will warm up and retain heat better. Just make sure the closed slide doesn't block major heating vents.

190   Insulate using rubber gym mats.

Interlocking rubber gym flooring mats come in handy as extra insulation and padding under your bed. They're especially valuable for pop-up campers or beds inside slideouts that are exposed more directly to the outside environment.

191   Use a portable propane heater when boondocking.

Stay warm while boondocking with a portable propane heater (like a Buddy). Since these work with radiant heat instead of using a blower fan (like with a furnace), they don't need battery power to stay warm. Just be sure to crack open a window slightly to ventilate the RV a bit for fresh air while in use.

◄ *Watchman Campground, Zion National Park, Utah /*
Photo © Julie Bennett

192 Maximize your solar power.

If you plan on doing a lot of boondocking with solar panels on your RV, maximize the hours you can draw power from the sun by installing solar panels with the option to tilt them (manually or electronically) as the sun moves throughout the day. Keeping your panels facing the sun provides substantially more power than if they are mounted flat on the roof. This isn't as much of a factor in summer as it is in winter, when the sun doesn't rise as high. Another cost-effective, flexible option is to add a portable solar panel that you can reposition throughout the day to maximize the benefit of solar rays.

193

Create a campsite lantern.

Wrap a headlamp around a translucent, water-filled bottle or jug (like a soda bottle or milk jug) with the light shining into the bottle to create a diffused lantern that provides light that is gentler, more comfortable, and less blinding than light from a bright headlamp.

194 Stay toasty with an inexpensive and lightweight DIY sleeping bag.

Buy two inexpensive, fuzzy polyester blankets of the same size (the kind you find at a dollar store). Sew them together along the bottom, and ⅔ of the way up on both of the two long sides. This will create a lightweight, budget-friendly, and roomy sleeping bag that is easy to wash and store. The polyester fabric does not breathe as much as natural fibers, so by sewing the edges together, the heat is held in better than with loose blankets. These are warm and cozy, and take up very little space and weight in the RV.

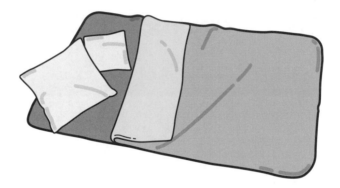

195 Save your RV light power.

If you have limited battery power when not hooked up to power, use battery-powered lanterns instead of your interior RV lights. Also switch your regular RV halogen or incandescent light bulbs to LED bulbs, which use less energy.

196 **Use fresh and gray water bladders.**

Dealing with water is usually the biggest limitation for longer stays on open land, so get a couple of large water bladders to avoid having to break camp. With a small pump, you can drain your RV gray tank into a bladder in the bed of your vehicle to take to town and dump. Then fill a separate, dedicated fresh water bladder to bring new water back to your camp. Just don't mix up the two bladders/auxiliary tanks!

197 **Reuse sink water.**

Don't fill your kitchen sink all the way for dishwashing. Just fill the sink halfway (or less), and when you're done washing, don't pull the drain plug. Leave the dirty water in the sink to presoak or prerinse the next day's dishes. You won't need nearly as much fresh, hot water in the sink to properly wash your dishes each time.

198 **Use paper towels to prewipe dirty dishes.**

Wipe down dirty dishes with a paper towel right after eating and before washing. This keeps smelly and greasy food particles out of your wastewater tanks, and allows you to use far less water when dishwashing, as the dishes are mostly clean. This will also help reduce food scraps and greasy gunk going down into your gray waste tanks, which can get smelly, especially on hot days.

199   Make your own toilet.

To really minimize black tank usage while out in the boonies, make your own dry toilet. Take a 5-gallon bucket, line the top with a sliced pool noodle for comfort, and hang a roll of toilet paper on the metal handle. Place a plastic bag across the opening, which will be secured by your weight when sitting on the pool noodles, to collect the solids. This way you can take care of business inside your van/RV, then dispose of it appropriately.

200   Dump your gray tanks without breaking camp.

If your campsite doesn't have a sewer connection and you don't want to carry a large portable waste tank on wheels, simply use a 5-gallon water jug with a large fill nozzle (or use a large funnel) to dump some of your gray wastewater into. Carry or drive it to the dump station so you don't need to break camp with your RV. It may require a few trips, depending on the size of your RV gray tank, but it's a compact and inexpensive solution.

201 Find your RV easily with a unique flag.

Mount a flagpole with a unique flag and/or LED lights to help you find your RV campsite, whether you're camping in a remote location or at an RV rally with hundreds of look-alike RVs. Most RV flagpoles can be mounted to the built-in ladder or hitch.

202 Save on power with electricity-free coffee making.

Save on power usage when making your coffee by using a French press coffee maker (like a BODUM) or an Italian-style stovetop coffee maker (like a MOKA), or boiling a kettle of water on the propane stove.

Chapter 4
RV LIVING

COOKING, ORGANIZATION, AND STORAGE

Looking for nifty ways to get organized and store things in your RV? What about budget-friendly RV makeover ideas? Or even tips for choosing the right RV for you? And how about creative solutions for easy meal planning in such a small space? Don't worry; we've got you covered in this chapter, where we share some of our favorite tips and best secrets for RV living.

Treat your first RV as a "learner" before investing more money.

203 **Start small and simple.**

Don't overinvest in your first RV—it will teach you the most about RV life and what you do and don't like in a floor plan and layout. Treat your first RV as a "learner" before investing more money in an RV that you believe will last you for the medium or long term.

204 **Rent before buying an RV.**

Don't make an expensive mistake buying an RV that doesn't work for you. Rent an RV first to get a feel for the size, drivability, floor plan, and layout, and to see whether or not you even like the lifestyle, before purchasing one. It's a great way to learn *fast* about what you like and what you don't. And the money you spend on renting can save you a lot more in the long run compared to buying the wrong RV, then taking a big financial hit when you go to sell it.

205 **Pretend in an RV before buying it.**

When you're shopping for RVs, try everything out in pretend mode. Pretend to wash dishes, eat from the dinette, sleep in the bed, take a shower, use the toilet, prepare a meal, watch the TV, work on your laptop—and make sure everything works for you before buying! If the RV has slideouts, bring all the slides *in* to make sure you can still access important areas—like the toilet, fridge, bed, and important cabinets, especially on travel days or if the slideout malfunctions.

206 **Chill out before your trip.**

Turn on your RV fridge the day before your trip to cool it down in advance. It can take many hours for an RV fridge to reach optimal operating temperature so it is safe for you to store your food.

◀ *Mountain road in Colorado / Photo © Julie Bennett*

207 Have your RV pay for itself.

If you use your RV only seasonally or for vacations, consider renting it out when you aren't using it to help offset your RV cost of ownership. If you have space on your property, you could set it up as an Airbnb rental. You could list it on a peer-to-peer RV rental platform like RVShare.com or Outdoorsy.com. Or if you want to avoid paying storage fees, list your RV with a management company that will take care of the rentals for you while keeping it stored at their location.

208 Keep your fridge cool while driving.

Place ice blocks from the freezer (or a plastic container with a frozen meal you want to defrost) inside your RV fridge to help keep everything cool when you turn off the fridge while driving. Put the ice blocks back in the freezer when you get to your destination so they are ready for next time.

209 Make foil packet meals.

Save on meal prep time and reduce dirty dishes by making foil packet meals to cook outside on your barbecue or campfire. It's a fun way to cook and serve individual meals outdoors, and you can eat right out of the foil packet, using a plate (regular or paper) as a solid base, if needed.

210 Line your barbecue with foil.

Line the lid and base of your barbecue with foil to keep it clean and looking like new longer.

211 Use all-purpose stainless steel cups.

Stainless steel tumblers can be used for all beverages—they keep hot drinks hot and cold drinks cold, and can be safely used inside or outside the RV. They won't break if you drop them, and they come with sealing lids to prevent spillage. Get a different color for everyone and never get your cups mixed up again. Simply rinse or clean as needed when you change your beverage. You'll save space by not needing extra cups or glasses, and you'll reduce waste from disposable cups.

212 Make a no-spill cup for travel days.

No lid for your cup and worried about spills? Cover the top of your beverage cup with Glad Press'n Seal plastic wrap and insert a straw to convert a regular cup into a travel-safe cup.

213

Have a meal ready on travel day to help things run smoothly.

Always have a simple meal ready (a premade dinner or leftovers are ideal) on travel days. You never know if you're going to encounter delays, and travel days always take longer than expected. This is one less thing to worry about when you arrive at your destination, and it helps prevent anyone onboard from getting hangry, or starting or ending the trip on a bad note.

214   **Store items in your oven.**

There's good space inside that oven, so use it for storing kitchen items, bowls, cookware—anything! Most propane ovens in RVs require lighting them from inside, which helps prevent accidentally heating them with something inside. Just make sure the oven is turned *off* and fully cooled first before storing anything. And before using, remove all items before turning it on.

215   **Save fridge space while keeping produce fresher longer.**

Maximize RV fridge space by storing fruits and vegetables in specialty bags (such as Debbie Meyer Green Bags) designed to keep produce fresh for longer, and you'll be able to fit more into fridge nooks and crannies. The flexible bags can fill wasted space better than rigid hard containers, so you can make the most of your small RV fridge or cooler.

216   **Balance heat distribution in your RV oven.**

Place a pizza stone or large ceramic tile inside your propane RV oven to keep the temperature more consistent while cooking.

217   **Pre-prepare one-pot meals in a zip-top bag.**

Before your camping trip, prepare several one-pot meals—say, for a pressure cooker, a slow cooker, or an air fryer—at home to save on time and washing up. Combine all ingredients—protein, vegetables, seasonings, sauces—into a zip-top bag, label with date and recipe name, and freeze flat. These meals will take up little space in the freezer. And when you're ready to make a meal in your RV, toss the ingredients into the appliance, set the timer, and go for a hike. Come back to a ready-made dinner and just one dirty pot to clean! Or throw everything into a skillet and cook on the stovetop.

218 Use plastic bottles in the fridge door.

Use BPA-free plastic bottles of the same size and shape instead of glass to store liquids on the fridge door shelf—think oils, vinegars, ketchup, mustard, sauces, condiments, marinades, and dressings. Bottles of the same size and shape will efficiently maximize the use of your fridge space and save on weight too. Plastic door shelves for an RV fridge are surprisingly expensive to replace when they break, and this hack will help reduce the likelihood of the shelf cracking under the weight.

219 Make less messy s'mores in a bag.

Add toasted marshmallows and a spoonful of chocolate chips to small bags of graham crackers—like Teddy Grahams. Mix it all together and eat your s'mores with a fork or spoon to avoid sticky fingers.

220 Store dinnerware safely outside.

When you're enjoying an outdoor meal, use a cake carrier on your table to protect disposable plates, paper napkins, and utensils from insects and dirt or to prevent them from flying off in the wind.

221 Increase counter space with a stovetop cover.

You can easily make a cover for your stove with a piece of wood that can double as a cutting board. Cover the bottom with felt or a layer of foam to help keep the stove grids from rattling as you drive.

222 Use silicone bags—for everything!

Food-grade silicone bags are reusable, lightweight, airtight, and space efficient, and they won't rattle! Use them to safely store food in the fridge, freezer, or pantry, and to reheat food in the microwave. You can also use them for storing electronics, pens and stationery items, and jewelry, and to seal up your wet swimsuits for transport after a dip in the pool. You can get them in different shapes, sizes, and colors for various uses.

223 Reuse high-quality food containers.

You can justify polishing off another pint of gelato when you wash and reuse that container for RV pantry storage! These round containers stack well, have tight-sealing lids, and are clear, so you can easily see the contents. The slight lip on the rim also makes it easy to stack more containers on top in the cupboard to take full advantage of vertical space.

224 Click and lock your storage containers.

Use a set of plastic storage containers with lids that can click and lock into bases so you can stack them. This allows you to maximize your storage space in the fridge and pantry and also helps prevent containers sliding around on travel days. Unused containers can stack, while unused lids snap together for more efficient storage. Buy a variety set of different sizes so you have the right size for the job and can make the most of your small RV fridge and pantry storage.

225   Invest in quality food storage containers.

The key to keeping produce fresh in your RV refrigerator is to protect against moisture and air. Having an excellent set of airtight containers will help you achieve this. Throw a dry paper towel into your containers to absorb moisture from your produce. Containers are also necessary for storing your dry goods to allow for better organization, maximize your storage, and protect them from mice that may get in (yikes!).

226   Cook one-pot meals to make mealtime easier.

One-pot meals are fast and easy, save on prep space and time, and reduce cleaning time and effort. When you're RV camping or cooking in a small space, the simpler and easier the meal, the better.

227   Line shelves to keep things quietly in place.

Line cupboard shelves and drawers with rubber grip liner—and even in between dishes—to reduce clanging and movement when traveling. The thicker, premium-quality grip liner works better than the cheaper, thin liner, which bunches up easily.

228

Keep a small fan in your fridge.

Install a small computer fan inside your RV fridge for better air circulation. Small computer fans are quiet and energy efficient, and they take up very little space. Circulating the air inside your RV fridge will significantly improve efficiency and temperature consistency to keep things nice and cool.

229   **Maximize fridge space on grocery hauls.**

Utilize every inch of refrigerator space by breaking down bulky food packaging after purchasing and before storing in the refrigerator. Food packaging such as spinach containers, fresh meat packaging, and cold cuts can condense down to a fraction of the space they are sold as. Transferring food into plastic or silicone bags or airtight food storage containers allows you to fully pack your refrigerator to the max and extend time between shopping trips. If you have your RV at the store, do this in the parking lot to take advantage of their trash and/or recycle bins.

CHRISTINE AND AARON WILLERS OF IRENEIRONFITNESS.COM

"Before hitting the road, our main staple for grocery shopping was Costco or Sam's Club. When we started our full-time RV life in our 22' Airstream Sprinter van, we knew no other way than to bulk shop! Our very first warehouse shopping trip resulted in us throwing everything on the floor because we had no idea how to store the big, bulky packages. Because we drive our van to the store, we have learned to take the time to unpack and get organized in the parking lot. We take items out of boxes and big plastic containers, then transfer food into silicone or plastic bags and storage containers that fit efficiently into our RV fridge and cupboard. We off-load our trash on-site at the store while there as a paying patron, instead of having to deal with it later at the campground or while out boondocking! Two years later, we have perfected our tiny van shopping escapades and still do mostly warehouse shopping to save money."

230   Monitor temperatures.

Mount thermometers with a remote temperature sensor to monitor temperatures inside and outside of your RV. Use one inside your fridge to ensure it stays cool enough for food safety without having to open the door. Some sensors even have alerts if the temperature drops out of a specified range. If you like Bluetooth technology, install a SensorPush thermometer/hygrometer to monitor temperature and humidity inside your RV, fridge, battery bay, and vehicle, then track, get alerts, and view the history. You can even add a Wi-Fi gateway to track it remotely from anywhere.

231   Use a magnetic knife rack to safely store sharp tools.

Securely mount a strong magnetic knife strip horizontally on your RV kitchen wall (not behind slides). Place knives on it vertically—handle up—to prevent them from sliding down when driving on bumpy roads. Your knives will be kept safely out of the way, and you'll free up valuable drawer space.

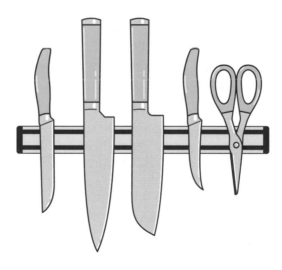

Ten Tips for RV Organization and Storage

232 Save space and clutter in the shower.

Install a wall-mounted dispenser in your shower for liquid soap, shampoo, and conditioner. It will keep things tidy and make for fewer items to put away on travel days. Plus, the clear panels show when it's time to refill them.

233 Roll up your clothes to fit more items.

Make the most of shallow RV drawer storage by rolling up shirts, pants, and other garments to save space, reduce wrinkles, and easily access items in your drawer without messing everything up. Create a shirt burrito by folding your shirts as you normally would, then grab the bottom of the folded shirt and roll the shirt up on itself. You'll fit many more rolled clothing items in your RV drawers.

234 Create a shoe storage footrest.

Put a box or basket in the passenger foot space area of motorhomes to store shoes and other items at the front of the RV when parked in a location. A lidded box can also double as a footrest for shorter passengers.

235 Keep your remotes together.

Keep remote controls stored in a drawer, or a basket or box with a lid, so they don't get lost or end up under the slides.

236 Use alternate containers as trash cans.

In small spaces like RV bathrooms and kitchens that don't have room for a trash can, use plastic storage containers in a size and shape that better fits your space.

237 Create wall storage with wire baskets.

Affix a row of Command hooks on the wall to hang a rectangular-shaped wire basket for holding a variety of items, including fruits and vegetables that can be stored at room temperature.

238 Stack, nest, and collapse to save space and weight.

Use stacking, nesting, and collapsible kitchenware—from bowls, measuring spoons, and measuring cups to collapsible lettuce spinners and dish drainers—to save space in your RV cupboards.

239 Reuse high-quality food containers.

Wash and reuse containers for RV pantry storage. Round gelato containers are clear, so you can easily see the contents, and the tight-sealing lids with a lip stack well, so you can maximize vertical space.

240 Maintain your kitchen organization.

Store smaller jars, bottles, condiments, and spices inside a clear plastic fridge or pantry organizer bin to keep things better organized. This will also prevent them from moving around while the vehicle is in motion.

241 Keep kitchen items in place.

Mount a towel rod at the back of your RV kitchen counter wall to keep often-used items like jars, canisters, and spices in place between the rod and the wall.

242 Cook outside as much as you can.

Cook outside of the RV as much as possible to keep mess, smell, and condensation to a minimum inside. You can use a barbecue grill outside, of course, but you can also set up a separate cooking table outside for cooking with electrical appliances such as a portable electric cooktop, air fryer, electric griddle, pressure cooker, slow cooker, or rice cooker. Plus, it's just more fun being outside immersed in your camping environment while cooking.

243 Prewash your fruit and vegetables.

Before you head out to camp off-grid, plan ahead and wash and dry your fruit and vegetables, either at home or in the campground; it will save on water usage while you're out boondocking.

244 Precook water-intensive foods in advance.

Prepare foods that use a lot of water to cook—like boiling pasta, rice, or eggs—in advance of a boondocking trip to save on water.

245 Freeze water in drink bottles for ice blocks.

Fill energy drink bottles, Tetra Pak packages, and wine bladders with water and freeze them. Just allow extra room in the top for the water to expand as it freezes. Use them in your fridge or cooler instead of bags of ice, as large ice blocks will keep items cold longer and the ice won't melt or cause a soggy mess. Pack frozen bottles to keep your food cool when heading out on picnics, and you can drink the cold water later as the ice melts. Keep the bottles (almost) filled and frozen in your home refrigerator so they are always ready to go.

▶ *Red Ants Pants Music Festival, White Sulfur Springs, Montana / Photo © Julie Bennett*

Cook outside of the RV to keep mess to a minimum inside.

246 Use clear plastic storage bins with tight lids.

Storing things in clear bins makes it easy to see the contents without opening them. They're especially useful for food storage, and a tight lid helps keep pests out.

247 Store spices on a cabinet door or in a pill organizer.

Mount spice bottle storage clips to the inside of a cupboard and snap in small plastic spice jars for easy storage and access. For an even more compact spice storage solution on short trips, fill a pill organizer, Tic Tac containers, or even small zip-top bags with your favorite spices. All these will save on money, space, and weight.

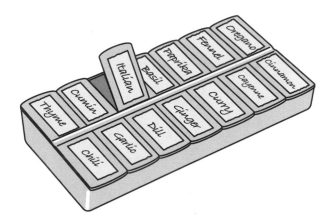

248 Keep it simple in the kitchen.

You don't need many tools to create an incredible meal. Determine which tools you use most often, and stick to them. For example, you can do a lot with a 10" skillet and a spatula, a pressure cooker, an outdoor griddle, or an air fryer. Pick just one or two gadgets that work for you, then use them frequently.

249   Prep all ingredients first.

Limited counter space in an RV can be challenging when you're cooking. Get all your necessary ingredients ready to go—washed, cut, and measured out. Having all of the bottles and bulky tedious work out of the way is critical for a smooth cooking experience. Once you are set up, flip open your stovetop lid and go into cook mode. It takes a little extra time up front to get organized, but you will be thankful when you're not dropping items, making a mess, or burning yourself!

250   Load up on the spices.

Even if you pare down your cooking appliances and tools to fit in an RV, you can still make food that tastes great. One secret is to maximize your use of spices to make foods flavorful and unique. Think of proteins and vegetables as your blank canvases and spices as your paint colors.

251   Embrace nonperishables.

When you're working with a small RV refrigerator with limited space, keep your eyes peeled for pantry staples that don't require refrigeration. Spices, vinegars, and hot sauces are great examples, along with shelf-stable produce items like onions, garlic, bell peppers, zucchini, and tomatoes. These are all safe to keep at room temperature and will maximize your vegetable intake even when your fridge is full.

252

Make durable, waterproof picnic table covers.

Step up from those flimsy and cheap outdoor tablecloths with generic prints that tear easily. Instead, buy some water-resistant fabric like oilcloth—online or from a fabric store—in a bright and happy color that suits your style. Cut to size and use as picnic tablecloths and bench covers. Attach to the table or bench seats with clamps or bungee cords to stop them from flying away in the wind. Oilcloth is easy to wipe down, fold, and store away, and because it is sturdier, it will last longer than the cheap tablecloths.

253

Use a waffle iron to make all kinds of fun meals.

You can use a waffle maker for more than just waffles, so use your imagination! It can do the job of multiple appliances, is space efficient, and keeps cleanup to a minimum. A waffle maker can replace a panini press, toaster, or toaster oven. Do a quick online search to find loads of inspiration and recipes. You can prepare batters in advance and take them with you on a camping trip; just pour onto a heated waffle iron for a quick and easy meal.

BRETT AND DANELLE HAYS

"We've become a big fan of the waffle iron, as it can be used for so many things! It all started when our RV oven wasn't working properly and we wanted corn bread to go with our bowl of chili. We decided to put corn bread batter in the waffle iron to see what happened and it turned out great! Next we decided to try brownie batter—that was a quick and easy dessert that we topped with ice cream. We never liked how the RV oven heated the place up anyway, so we rarely use it anymore. We just keep having fun experimenting with the waffle maker. Recently, we used it for Thanksgiving leftovers. The stuffing was dry, so we added some water and put it in the waffle maker. That turned out to be a great base for a delicious Thanksgiving leftover open-faced sandwich, topped with turkey, gravy, and cranberry sauce. Since then, we've used the waffle iron with pancake batter, cake batter, cinnamon rolls in a tube, hash browns, and bacon. The possibilities are endless! It has become so useful—now we have a good excuse for hauling it around."

254   Avoid slipping in wet baths.

If your RV has a wet bath, put a teakwood mat on the base of your wet bath floor to prevent slipping, standing on a wet floor, and tracking water through the RV. The wood mat dries fairly quickly and looks and feels a bit like you're at a spa! But if you are tall, keep in mind the height of the wood mat will also remove a couple inches of headroom.

255   Use Command hooks and Velcro everywhere.

Avoid drilling holes in your RV, and instead use removable Command hooks and/or Velcro for hanging everything from jackets and keys to decor and artwork in your RV. To ensure they hold securely and don't come loose on travel days, use a higher weight capacity for the hooks than the item you are hanging. You can also use industrial-strength Velcro for maximum hold, but that's not as easily removable so be careful where you use it if you want to remove it later.

256   Update your RV with peel-and-stick wallpaper.

Use removable, peel-and-stick wallpaper as an easy and inexpensive way to brighten and personalize your space. It's easy to apply, and it leaves no residue when you remove it. Use it on RV walls, as backsplash instead of tile, on cupboard and drawer faces, or even to hide unwanted mirrors. Freshen up your space, add accent colors, and give your RV a whole new look on a budget—to suit your changing style or seasons—while saving on weight. Wallpaper can also protect the RV walls and should be easy to remove if you want to restore your RV to its original state when it comes time to sell it.

257   **Use peel-and-stick tile for backsplashes.**

Real tile can be heavy and more likely to chip or break. If you want something more substantial than wallpaper behind your kitchen and bathroom sinks, use peel-and-stick tiles—they are lightweight, reasonably priced, and easy to apply, and they look great.

258   **Decorate using vertical spaces to minimize counter clutter.**

Counter space is limited in RVs, and it can be a pain putting things away on travel days. Aim to hang most of your art and personal decor touches on vertical spaces to create charm without the clutter. Use removable Command hooks that won't damage walls. Avoid hanging items on walls that go behind a slideout unless they are narrow enough to have clearance and are mounted really securely so they can't fall down and potentially get jammed in the slide.

259   **Place adhesive kitchen towel hooks in convenient locations.**

Use inexpensive adhesive towel hooks designed to "grab" kitchen towels (or washcloths in the bathroom) to keep them in spots that are easy to access while also keeping them in place on travel days.

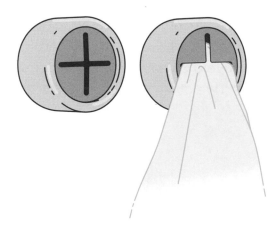

260 Use steel T-pins to hang art on carpet walls.

An RV with carpeted walls makes it difficult, if not impossible, to use Velcro or Command hooks for hanging things. Instead use T-pins to loop through a hook or loop on the back of your artwork or decor, then push the pin through the carpet and straight down to keep your decor securely affixed.

261 Use everyday decor to change up your RV.

Keep your RV decor base palette neutral and update it seasonally with colorful or themed items that are inexpensive and easy to change out. Items like kitchen towels, bathroom towels, photos, cushions and pillows, throw rugs, colored vases or plant pots, and even books can create your desired vibe or theme. You can also change up your RV style to complement locations you visit (e.g., nautical theme for beach or lake) or to celebrate seasonally for summer, fall, or holidays.

262 Decorate for holidays without the stuff.

Decorate your RV for the holidays simply and inexpensively. Use pine cones from your campsite, use a roll of wrapping paper and/or ribbon from a dollar store to decorate cabinet doors so they look like gifts, hang LED lights that can change color to suit any occasion, buy a pumpkin and gourds at the supermarket in the fall, or pick up a holiday bouquet from the local supermarket to use as a centerpiece. These items will help you avoid carrying holiday decor with you and save on space and weight, yet they still make sure you feel festive.

263 Use tension rods to keep things in place.

Keep things from falling forward in the fridge or on shelves with small curtain tension rods. You can also add Velcro dots at the ends for some extra "grab" to keep the rods in position when the RV is rolling down the road.

264 Create additional wardrobe storage.

Increase the storage capacity inside your clothes closet by hanging wire shelving inside on Command hooks and adding cube storage bins or baskets to store your nonhanging clothes, shoes, and other items. Simply cut the shelves to your desired length, affix four Command hooks to the closet side walls (and an extra one or two at the back if the shelf is long), then hook the shelves onto it. This is a great way to create removable shelves without drilling holes into your RV. Keep the wire shelf lip facing down to easily slide the cubes and baskets forward. Or flip with the shelf lip facing up to prevent boxes sliding forward on travel days. You can position the shelves exactly where you want them, and easily move them if you need to. It's a great way to create shelves at exactly the right height to maximize unused space in a closet without the need for drilling holes.

265 Change up your interior RV doors.

Replace your interior sliding, pocket, or traditional doors to give your space a modern look. Create your own design or hop on the Internet for inspiration to create this easy and affordable swap. Once your lightweight door is built, just use the existing hardware for an easy installation. If you have a plain door and you don't want to swap it, you can dress it up with an adhesive wall or door mural so it looks like art.

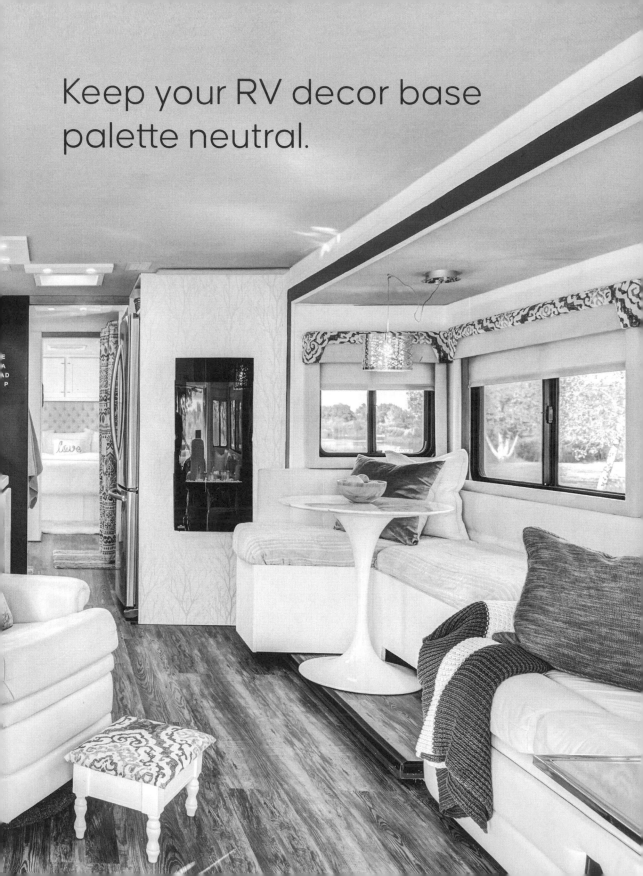

Keep your RV decor base palette neutral.

266 Swap out RV hardware.

Most RV hardware and fixtures can be swapped out for residential-style hardware. This will update the style of a space and make your RV feel more like a traditional home. Adapters may be needed in some circumstances, but in most scenarios this is an easy installation. Updated faucets, lighting, and cabinet hardware can completely transform a space without breaking your back or the bank.

MARISSA AND NATHAN MOSS OF LESSJUNKMOREJOURNEY .COM

"The best part of traveling with an RV is having your own space with you everywhere you go. But that doesn't mean your space has to feel like an RV. When we decided to move into an RV and travel full-time, we desired a space that felt like home. Unfortunately, some RVs can appear dark and outdated, and we needed a solution. We grabbed our paintbrush and toolbox and decided to give our RV a makeover. We painted the walls to brighten up the space, replaced the sliding doors with lightweight barn doors, and swapped out the flooring and window treatments—all of which has made our house on wheels feel like a 'home.' It is amazing what a huge impact even small changes can make in a tiny space. Having our home reflect our personality gave us a sense of familiarity anywhere we were camped in the country. We went from just RV camping to having a home on wheels, and for our family, that made all the difference in the world. Don't be afraid to make those changes and updates so home can be anywhere you park it."

◀ *Photo © GabrielaPhoto.com*

267 **Avoid rattling or broken bottles on travel days.**

Save your oils, vinegars, and other bottles from rattling, breaking, or tipping over on travel days. Slip each bottle and jar inside a Koozie to keep them protected. Or keep a stash of folding cardboard six-pack holders on hand to store and separate bottles. Another idea is to keep those reusable six-bottle divided tote bags (like you get from the liquor or grocery store) for wine bottles, vinegar, and oil bottles. They will keep the glass apart so they don't rattle and clang together, and they will also prevent them from falling over and making a mess. Plus they make it easier to carry bottles and jars and move them around.

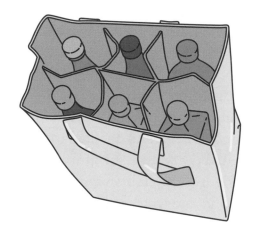

268 **Get more elbow room in the shower.**

Replace a straight rod with an Extend-A-Shower curtain rod that expands in and out. If you have a glass shower, you may be able to remove the doors and metal surround, keep the shower pan, and add the extendable rod and shower curtain to give you more space to lather up.

269 Hang wet clothes to dry in your shower.

Place a tension rod inside your shower to hang wet swimsuits, towels, jackets, and raincoats so they can drip down the drain while drying. Mount the rod in between walls and not glass, if possible, to avoid putting pressure on the glass and popping it out of its frame.

270 Use your shower as a mudroom.

Rinse off muddy shoes and boots, and leave them to dry on the shower floor or in a boot tray so they are out of the way. This will keep your floors clean, dry, and protected.

271 Use packing cubes for space-saving storage.

Use travel packing cubes for packing and organizing clothes and personal gear, using a different color for each family member. You'll maximize storage in your RV cupboards and drawers while making it easy for everyone to quickly find what they need. Use different sizes of packing cubes for clothes, shoes, books, toys, crayons, electronics, and even dry snacks like muesli bars in each person's preferred color. For day trips, pack one cube per person for their personal items and pop into your backpack; you'll quickly know whose stuff is whose when you need it.

272 Keep a stash of plastic shower caps.

Pick up some cheap plastic shower caps at a dollar store and use them to cover plates and protect your food from insects when outdoors. Or, slip them over wet or muddy shoes and hiking boots to avoid messes in your RV.

273   Create a tidy closet.

Sick of your clothes hangers falling down in your RV closet on drive days? Place a piece of flexible, ribbed black plastic tubing (ask for "split loom tubing" at the hardware store) across your closet rack bar. The grooves in the tubing will help prevent clothes hangers from sliding around or even falling off during RV road trips. Wire hangers are more effective for staying in place, as the narrow hooks drop down into the grooves better.

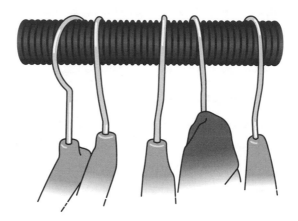

274   Don't go crazy buying new containers for your RV.

First, search your home for any storage containers that you might already own that will fit into your RV. Most RV cabinets, closets, and storage areas have very unique sizes and shapes, so you may need to find a variety of containers that will fulfill your needs. After you have exhausted the storage options you already have, fill in the voids by shopping for specific sizes and shapes that will make the most efficient use of your RV storage space.

275

Light up your space without wiring.

Mount battery-powered touch lights or motion sensor lights with Command strips, Velcro, or flush-mount magnets to give you light inside your closet, pantry, basement bays, outside—anywhere you want or need it—without wiring anything electrical. Some lights are even rechargeable via USB and don't need batteries.

276 Use hanging shoe storage to contain just about anything.

Made of fabric, plastic pockets, and metal hooks, hanging shoe storage products are lightweight and easy to hang. Toiletries, linens, clothing accessories, tools, office supplies, and other small objects will nestle neatly into each compartment. Organize by type of item and opt for clear pockets so you can quickly spot what you need. Making use of your walls and the backs of doors is a great way to expand your storage without cluttering your closet or floor space. Plus, these sell for under $15 and take seconds to install. To keep them from swaying on bumpy roads, secure with heavy-duty staples, Velcro, or Gorilla Tape.

MIKE AND ANNE HOWARD OF HONEYTREK.COM AND AUTHORS OF *ULTIMATE JOURNEYS FOR TWO* AND *COMFORTABLY WILD*

"With just 104 square feet of living space in Buddy the Camper, we had to get creative with our storage solutions. Once the cabinets and closet (yes, there's just one) were full in our Toyota Sunrader, we looked for ways to utilize bare walls and doors... and a hanging shoe rack was just the ticket! We found a clear-pocket design backed with a pretty fabric, which meant it was nice enough to display and easy to cut to the dimensions of each space. In the bathroom, the various compartments hold toiletries, jewelry, and first-aid supplies. By the front door, it organizes everything we'd need for a day outdoors—such as sunblock, bug spray, headlamp, hat, keys, etc.—so we can just grab and go."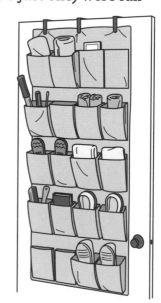

277 **Hang and clip supplies in the shower.**

Connect clear vinyl name badge clips to shower curtain rings and use the clips to hold small bathroom items like tubes of toothpaste or lotions. This keeps items out of other drawers and shelves and helps them stay put.

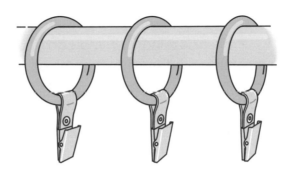

278 **Hide your toilet smells.**

Nobody likes stinky smells in a small space like an RV, so for odor control, use a septic-safe RV toilet tank treatment product (we like Happy Campers). This can do a surprisingly good job of containing smells in your RV toilet black tank and even your gray tanks. Yes, that dirty sink water can start smelling bad from rotting food or other debris in the tank. If your tanks get extra stinky on hot days, add some extra treatment to control it. Poo-Pourri for toilets can also minimize smells, both during your bathroom visit and while your deposits rest in the waste tank below.

279 **Use the shower area for multipurpose storage.**

Use the shower area as secondary storage for quilting supplies, craft supplies, coats, and other items. This can be used as a temporary or permanent storage solution, especially if you don't use the RV bathroom for taking showers and prefer using campground facilities instead.

280 Find anything in your RV.

It can be easy to lose track of items, especially in exterior basements of large RVs! Store items in translucent plastic bins with an itemized list. For each bin, print a list of its contents and place the list inside, facing out, so it's visible through the plastic. Creating lists on your computer makes them easy to read and update as needed. The biggest benefit is you don't have to go searching to find what you're looking for. Simply go to your computer to pull up the comprehensive list of all your bins and their contents. Do a word search for the item you're looking for to find the specific bin and location. Then go directly to the bin to find exactly what you need.

PETER KNIZE AND JOHN SULLIVAN OF THERVGEEKS.COM AND HOSTS OF *THE RVERS* TV SHOW

"Being full-time RVers and eager to handle our own repair and maintenance tasks ourselves, we keep a lot of 'stuff' on board. Our storage areas are filled with tools, spare parts, and supplies, making it a challenge to put our hands on the exact items we would need. The most frustrating experience of all is to search unsuccessfully, give up and go out and buy something, and then discover a few months later that we did have that part on board but couldn't find it. We made a big improvement to our organizational system by buying translucent plastic bins for our basement storage areas, and handwriting lists of the contents. This allowed us to quickly see what was in each bin without opening them. But we still had to physically look at each bin's list to see the contents. Our follow-up solution improved our system further by keeping the contents of each bin, and the associated lists, on our computer. Now we can simply search the master document for the name of the part, tool, or any supplies we're looking for, and the bin and its location come right up on the screen. And whenever a list changes, it's a snap to print out a new one."

281   **Install a curtain rod without drilling holes.**

Stick a couple of Command hooks on the wall near your window, then place a lightweight rod on the hooks for a super-versatile curtain rod you can install anywhere without drilling holes.

282   **Make a clock art piece to keep track of time.**

Make a style statement with a practical purpose by creating your own time zone art piece to keep track of the time in different parts of the country or world. Buy battery-operated digital or analog clocks—one for each time zone you want to display (four for North America, or more if you want to include an international city or two). Mount them to a board to hang on the wall or on the front of an RV cabinet door. Make a label for each time zone to mount underneath each clock, or have trophy plates engraved. This is useful for RVers who travel widely or have family and friends in other parts of the country or world to easily check the time anywhere, and it's a great conversation piece for guests!

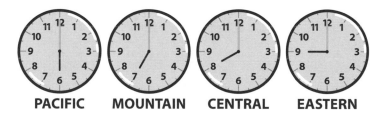

PACIFIC   MOUNTAIN   CENTRAL   EASTERN

283

Do weight training with what you have.

Instead of carrying bulky and heavy gym weights to work out with on camping trips, use cans of food or water-filled bottles for light-duty weight training. They may be lighter, but just increase your reps! Use your own body weight or bring a bag of elastic rubber resistance bands for portable fitness training on the go.

284 Freeze your smelly trash.

Place smelly trash like fish or meat in a bag and freeze it until you can get to a dumpster. This will reduce smells in your RV, especially in warm weather, and won't attract wildlife by leaving it outside.

285 Have dinner by "candlelight" safely.

Use LED battery-operated candles instead of regular flame candles to avoid the risk of fire and the buildup of soot stains on the ceiling of your RV. If you can, get the ones that use rechargeable batteries to reduce waste.

286 Keep your RV cool in summer.

In the heat of summer, an RV can struggle to keep the inside cool at times. Here are a few ways to help your RV's air conditioner. 1) Try to park the RV in a shaded area if possible. Shade from trees does wonders for the temperature inside your RV. 2) Use your awning on the sunny side to shade and cool the RV. 3) Keep your AC filters clean. Dirty filters lower the efficiency of the AC unit. 4) Cook meals outside whenever possible to reduce heat buildup in the rig. 5) Where possible, open opposing windows to take advantage of a cross breeze.

287 Bring an extra room.

Use a portable outdoor screen room to increase your living space outside, avoid bugs, and shelter from direct sun. This is especially useful if you have a smaller RV, have kids, or like to work or eat outside. They are usually very easy to set up and take down and can fold down into a small space for compact travel.

288 Double up your shoe storage.

Stash flip-flops and sandals inside boots and larger shoes. This not only increases your shoe storage space, but also holds up the tops of your boots—no shoe trees required.

EMILY ROHRER OF OWNLESSDOMORE.US

"Under traditional living conditions, my footwear collection of twelve pairs of shoes hardly merits notice. In fact, I can hear the girlfriend chorus screeching, 'You only have twelve pairs of shoes? How do you even survive?' But in an RV—even a larger fifth wheel like ours—twelve pairs of shoes seems excessive. Do I really need four pairs of boots? Well, no. The sassy riding and cowgirl boots are not wardrobe essentials, but I do wear them as occasions and outfits warrant. The hiking boots? Definitely essential for outdoor exploration. The snow boots? Well, if we planned our travels better during the winter months, I'd be able to pitch those, but I've worn them at least once or twice each year and been grateful I've kept them around. Surprisingly, it took until our fourth year on the road—and our second RV—for me to come up with a better shoe storage solution: nesting. When space is limited, fill the spaces that exist. So I stuck my sandals in my boots, and my shelf space doubled. *Ta-daaaa!* So although it may be true that you can't fill the voids in your life by buying shoes, you can fill the voids in your shoes with...more shoes!"

289   **Hang towels with an S hook.**

Use a simple S hook to hang your towels from your shower curtain rod for better drying and space efficiency. By hanging freely instead of against a wall, your towels will dry faster and won't take up extra space.

290   **Store instead of stow.**

When camping seasonally in the same area year after year—like snowbirds or sunbirds—you may find you end up carrying "stuff" on board all year that you use only seasonally. Instead of cramming all your stuff into cupboards and basements and schlepping it around with you everywhere you go, rent a small storage unit in your seasonal area while you're away and just take what you need for your travels the rest of the year.

Chapter 5

WORK AND TECHNOLOGY ON THE ROAD

You may be traveling in an RV, but unless you can *really* get away from it all, you'll need Internet access. You might be a tech nomad, remote worker, or an RV entrepreneur. Or maybe you roadschool your kids, look for entertainment on the go, or want to stay in touch with family and friends. These hacks will keep you connected on the road.

Find your
perfect work-
life balance.

291   **Take power on the go.**

Carry a small portable device charger to take with you on hikes and outings so you always have power for your devices when needed, especially if you rely on them for directions. For longer trips, use a larger portable battery-charging station for electronics, especially when camping off the grid without power. Charge power stations when you're plugged into power at home or at a campground, and then use them to recharge your devices multiple times when on the go.

292   **Use one screen in multiple places.**

Save space and gain more flexibility by installing mounts for your iPad or tablet in multiple locations in the RV. Get special mounts, or simply place a Velcro strip on the back of your device and another strip on any walls you want. This reduces the need for multiple TVs in your small space, and you won't have to watch TV from a fixed location. You can even install a screen mount in the dash area to use your iPad for GPS navigation.

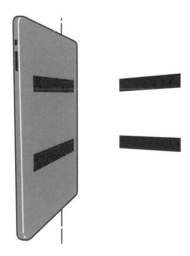

◀ *Humboldt Redwoods State Park, California / Photo © Marc Bennett*

293 Carry a small library instead of one book.

Use a digital reader like Kindle, Kobo, or NOOK to download and read several books instead of bringing a pile of paper books. Or download audio books from Audible.com to listen to on your smartphone, tablet, or computer. These will give you more reading and entertainment options while saving on weight and space as you travel.

294 Charge your devices faster.

Your devices will charge much faster when you put your smart-phone and tablet into Airplane Mode when they are plugged in.

295 Find work and even a free campsite by being a Workamper.

Want to stay busy, meet people, make (or save) money, and work while you roam? Find part-time, full-time, or seasonal positions around the country that pay, offer a free campsite, or both! Use your skills to be a Workamper at RV parks, camp-grounds, national parks, state parks, marinas, dude ranches, and more at Workamper.com and WorkampingJobs.com. Get in plenty of steps and potential bonuses over the holiday sea-son by joining Amazon CamperForce and working in one of the program's warehouses. Get physical up north in the fall har-vesting beets at one of many locations (www.theunbeetable experience.com). Find seasonal jobs in nursing around the country in snowbird locations. Or follow the weather—and the demand—with construction jobs as you travel.

296

Get packages delivered safely.

Some campgrounds and RV parks don't accept mail or package deliveries, so always check before placing orders or forwarding mail. If you want to receive United States Postal Service (USPS) mail, address it with your name and have it sent to "General Delivery" at a local USPS location, where it will be held for up to 2 weeks. You can also have your UPS and FedEx packages sent to their local respective stores for a small fee per box upon pickup. Send your Amazon orders to a local Amazon Hub Locker or Amazon Hub Counter for pickup. An Amazon Prime account will get you free 2-day shipping for most items and locations.

297 Create an office in the cockpit to use when you're parked.

In motorhomes, the driver and passenger areas and seats can be used as a comfortable, ergonomic workspace when parked. Creative solutions may involve using the steering wheel and front dash along with flip-up desks, folding tables, or lap desks. If you have a Class A motorhome, tilt the steering wheel up as far as it goes and place a board on top for your laptop, with some rubbery shelf liner underneath to keep it in place. Work from the driver's seat with a lap desk, wireless keyboard, and mouse—you'll have an excellent workspace with a view while keeping your work out of the main living space. On the passenger side, use or modify the front dash area to place a laptop or mount a monitor. Or spin the seats around 90–180 degrees and mount a monitor, install a flip-up desk, or use a folding desk for a space-efficient cockpit office when parked in a location.

298   **Digitize your life.**

Instead of carrying paper documents, files, receipts, and other records, go digital instead. Make digital copies of paper documents with a scanner or use an app like TurboScan to store digital documents in the cloud or on a hard drive. It will take up less space and weight, and help keep you more organized.

299   **Save your battery with Airplane Mode.**

If your phone or tablet battery is running low and you need it later, put your device into Airplane Mode. This uses less battery power than turning it off and back on again, and many features and apps will still be available to use. A phone that is constantly searching for signal in a low coverage area will drain the battery faster. When you turn off Airplane Mode, the phone will automatically search for a cellular tower.

300   **Leave your printer at home!**

With so many digital programs available for converting and signing documents, there is a reduced need for printing. Most people rarely need to print much for work these days, especially when working from an RV instead of an office. If you work from the road, or occasionally have a need to print and sign paper documents, you probably don't need to bring a printer in your RV. Simply save the file to a USB memory stick and take it (or email it) to a Staples or FedEx location or other local printing shop, where they can print your pages quickly and inexpensively.

301 Find your perfect work-life balance.

If you have flexibility, be intentional about your work hours. Track exactly when you're actually working so you have a realistic picture of your total time spent on the job. Then ask yourself if that reality is working for you, and make adjustments as needed. It is important to know when it's time to shut the computer down and enjoy this lifestyle you've created for yourself!

HEATH PADGETT OF THERVENTREPRENEUR.COM AND HEATHANDALYSSA.COM

"The hardest part about working and traveling in an RV is feeling like you're spending too much time in front of the laptop. Work-life balance, especially for RV entrepreneurs, is a constant battle. It's easy to feel like you're working too much or playing too much. Everyone is different, so the key is finding what works for you. I asked myself: How many hours do I need to work to support my family? How many hours make me feel like I'm working too much to enjoy life? I came up with a range of numbers and wrote it on a Post-it and stuck it on my computer. This reminds me to stick to the parameters I created for myself. If your work is keeping you from enjoying your travels, then there isn't much point to traveling while you work!"

302 Dry out a water-damaged phone.

Turn the phone off and place it in a zip-top bag filled with uncooked, dry rice or silica gel packets—like the ones that come in vitamin bottles—and leave it untouched for 48 hours before turning it on again.

▶ *Middlefork RV Park, Fairplay, Colorado / Photo © Marc Bennett*

Pay attention to campground names for coverage clues.

303 **Prevent ads from interrupting your games and draining battery power.**

When playing games on your smartphone or tablet, put the device into Airplane Mode to prevent those annoying ads from popping up.

304 **Remember and protect your passwords.**

Use an encrypted password manager like LastPass or Dashlane to remember your passwords, and log in and out using your master password every time you use it. If your device is ever lost or stolen, as long as you're logged out, no one will have easy access to secure sites and your passwords.

305 **Use toy haulers for things other than toys.**

When shopping for RVs with more flexible space options, consider toy hauler floor plans for use beyond just hauling toys. Convert the large, open toy hauler room into a mobile office space, a craft room, or an extra bedroom. If you are creative with how you do it, you may still be able to use the space to transport your toys and large items, unload them when you arrive at your destination, then set up the room for your alternate use.

306 **Set a designated workspace and schedule.**

If possible, designate one area of your RV as your mobile office. If you are using a dual area, like your dinette, try to set designated work hours when you use the dinette as your office versus as your dining room. Dedicate a cabinet to storing your computer, files, and any work gadgets after hours so they are out of sight and allow you to switch off.

307 Convert a bunk area into an office.

Convert an RV bunkhouse into a dedicated office to close off from the rest of the RV for increased privacy and productivity.

MARC BENNETT OF RVLOVE.COM AND CO-AUTHOR OF *LIVING THE RV LIFE* **AND** *RV HACKS*

"When we first decided to hit the road in an RV, I had a full-time remote job. Work-life balance and good ergonomics are important to me, so I wanted a dedicated work area that I could close off at the end of the day. We specifically bought a motorhome with a bunkhouse floor plan so we could convert the bunk area into an office. We removed the top bunk bed, installed a desktop and mounted a keyboard tray underneath, and put in an ergonomic office chair. It already had two bookshelves at the end of each bunk area, which I used to store work-related files and gear. We added a tension rod and curtains along the side of the bunk room, so when the work day was over, I simply pulled the curtains to hide the office away. This allowed me to really switch off from work, which was fantastic for maintaining better work-life balance. I even had a window with a changing view every time we moved!"

308

Get everyone headphones to keep the peace.

With a set of headphones for everyone in the RV, noise is contained when anyone is watching TV, playing games, or listening to music or podcasts. This makes it easier to maintain peaceful and harmonious cohabitation in a small space. Large over-ear headphones work especially well—since they are more visually obvious, you can easily see when others are occupied.

309 Keep an office hidden under your bed.

Many RVs have a bed that lifts up to access under-bed storage. As the bed isn't generally used in the day, create a stealthy workspace by lifting the bed and installing a drop-down desk under the platform base that gets put away at night. With creative modifications, you could set up an entire office space with a desktop for your laptop, mouse, and keyboard, and even a flip-down monitor. Use a folding chair or one that can move out to the living area at night. This is a great use of space, assuming you and your partner's sleeping schedules are aligned.

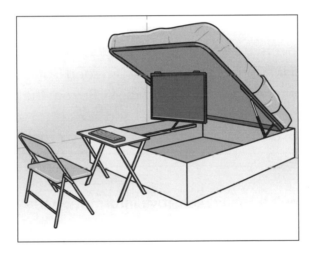

310 Discover ways to make money while you explore.

For travelers and explorers, passive income is one of the best ways to support life on the road. Make money while you sleep by selling digital products online, such as ebooks or online courses. Create systems so your business runs without you, such as outsourcing the shipping of physical products. This allows you to keep making money and growing your business while you're out doing more fun stuff like exploring national parks.

311 Use your main driving vehicle as a private office.

If you're working remotely from the RV and need to join a Zoom meeting or make a private call, head out to your main driving vehicle and use it as a separate, private office space. This is especially handy if you have kids or if two people are working remotely.

312 Find free Wi-Fi.

Use free public Wi-Fi to connect to the Internet and use apps (those that don't use personal data) while minimizing data usage on your cellular plan as you travel. You can usually find free Wi-Fi at many campgrounds, libraries, coffee shops, restaurants, hotels, museums, and even some city parks. Popular chains with free Wi-Fi include McDonald's, Starbucks, Panera Bread, Apple, Best Buy, and Barnes & Noble. You may even be able to connect to Wi-Fi from the parking lot (after you've made a purchase) and work from your car or RV. You can also find Wi-Fi hotspots near you using apps like WiFi Finder.

313 Don't transmit sensitive information through free Wi-Fi.

Keep in mind public Wi-Fi networks are open, not secure, and therefore risky. So don't use one for too long and definitely not for sensitive online activity like online banking.

314 Protect yourself from hackers and stay secure online with a VPN.

If you're on public networks frequently, consider subscribing to a VPN (virtual private network) service to browse the web privately as you travel. It will enable you to feel more comfortable using public Wi-Fi hotspots, and will help prevent hackers from stealing your data when you're online.

315 Watch movies for free or cheap.

Many campgrounds have a library with DVDs that you can borrow and watch in your RV (the same goes for books, puzzles, and games). You can also rent DVDs inexpensively from Redbox in one location and return them to a Redbox at your next destination. Watching DVDs instead of streaming saves on cellular data usage too.

316 Stay in your office's time zone to avoid confusion.

Adjust the settings on your computer so it stays set to your main work location's time zone and doesn't adjust automatically, regardless of where you are traveling. It helps you stay on track with meetings while also time-stamping your emails in the same time zone as your boss and colleagues. (It also helps keep your location a secret if you don't want it to be known you're traveling!) If your work and travel time zones are completely opposite—say, Pacific versus Eastern—keep *all* of your clocks set to your work time zone so you can operate completely within that schedule—it will be less mentally confusing and less disruptive to your body.

317 Set your time zone manually to avoid international charges and unwanted time zone switches.

If you are staying near the border of a state that has a time zone change, turn off the feature that automatically sets the date and time on your phone, and manually select your preferred time zone. This will prevent confusion if your phone bounces between cellular towers, potentially changing time zones back and forth. It's also a good idea to do this if you're traveling alongside country borders (Canada and Mexico). And you will avoid possible international charges if your phone jumps to a cellular tower on the other side.

Top Apps for Staying Connected

318 WiFi Finder, Wi-Fi Map.

Use these apps to find free Wi-Fi locations everywhere you go.

319 Coverage?

Check for cellular coverage maps across multiple carriers in one handy app.

320 Speedtest by Ookla.

Quickly test the speed and performance of your Internet connection anywhere in the world on all your devices.

321 Find My.

Keep track of your family members' Apple devices—even if they are offline—with this handy app.

322 Surfshark VPN.

This is a useful tool for keeping your Internet connection secure and accessing all your favorite content online.

323 Life360.

This app has various plans that allow you to keep track of family members' location, driving, and digital safety—and get alerts in case of an accident.

324 RV LIFE, Campendium.

Check campground reviews with reports on cellular connectivity for major carriers using these handy apps.

325 Facebook.

Meet like-minded people and get support in RV-friendly groups like Internet for RVers & Cruisers, The RV Entrepreneur, Living the RV Life, and many others based on a variety of RV topics (RV type, pets, newbies, full-time RVing, RV decorating, etc.).

326 Instagram.

Find and follow other RVers sharing their adventures, get ideas and inspiration on where to camp, learn, and connect online or meet up in person.

327 Nomad Near Me.

Connect with fellow travelers with shared interests or get alerts to know when friends are in the area.

328

Enable your GPS location so emergency contacts know where you are.

It's a good idea for loved ones to know where you are, so add a family member, friend, or emergency contact to an app that will always show your geographic location. Use the "Share your location" feature on Google Maps, Apple's Find My app, or apps like Glympse or Life360.

329 Use hard drive backups to save data.

Use a portable hard drive for storing and backing up your files instead of relying on the cloud. When you're traveling, this will increase the dependability of accessing the data you need, especially if you are in areas where cellular coverage isn't strong. Using a hard drive instead of the cloud will also significantly reduce your data usage to help you avoid hitting the data cap limit on your cellular plan. You can always upload or back up your files to cloud storage again when you get back to your home Internet.

330 Look for unexpectedly strong cell signals in small towns.

Surprisingly, some of the best cellular connections can be found in small towns and remote areas where there are fewer people sharing a cell tower. You may even be able to park your RV closer to a cellular tower for an even stronger and faster connection. Keep in mind, though, that if it's the only tower in town and something goes wrong, all coverage may drop.

331 Save on data usage when streaming.

Avoid 4K and HD when you're streaming videos and instead change the resolution setting to SD or even down to 360p to dramatically reduce your total data usage. The video will start quicker and stream better when your connection is weak, and the video quality will still be good enough to watch. Also turn off the feature to automatically play video on *Facebook* and other apps. Many so-called unlimited plans with cellular providers are not truly unlimited and will only stream full speed for a limited amount of data, often under 25–30GB. After that, they will deprioritize your connection by slowing your speed when the network is congested, or throttle your data speed completely once you've hit your monthly data allowance until you hit your next billing cycle.

332 Slow the data suck by turning off automatic syncing.

Turn off automatic syncing among your devices (phones, tablets, computers) and manually back up your photos and video to a hard drive—or to the cloud only when you're back on a Wi-Fi connection. If you have multiple devices that automatically sync among each other, it will suck your cellular data up very quickly, especially if you like to take lots of photos and video of the amazing locations you visit. Check your phone's settings to see which apps use the most cellular data, then delete apps you don't use, turn off notifications you don't need, and disable location settings unless they are necessary, or change them so that they're accessed only when using the app. Saving on data usage can help you avoid hitting your monthly data cap limit or incurring overage charges on your cellular plan.

333 Understand your cell plan's data plan.

As you dive into selecting cellular data plans, you'll quickly realize that your definition of *unlimited* is different from the carriers'. Many plans place limiting caps on mobile hotspot data—the type of data you'd use to get a laptop or smart TV online. Most streaming services have apps where you can watch your favorite shows right on your smartphone or tablet, and with many cellular plans this kind of on-device data really *is* unlimited. Bonus tip: Get an adapter that allows you to use an HDMI output from your phone or tablet, and you can view your content on a larger TV!

334 Do your downloads in advance.

Plan ahead for your trip and download music, podcasts, audiobooks, games, and videos to your devices (phone, tablet, computer) at home when you are connected to Wi-Fi to save on data usage while traveling.

335 Watch small-town event calendars in order to avoid cell usage spikes.

If Internet speed and reliability are important to you, avoid destinations hosting a big event that will cause huge spikes in population, unless that's the reason you plan to be there, of course! These temporary increases in population size in smaller towns can overload the existing cell tower infrastructure that is set up to support the average population. You may find yourself with a great connection initially, only to find the cell tower soon becomes overloaded to the point where you can't even send a simple text message—in which case, forget about work and go have fun, or move to another location.

336 Research mobile Internet redundancy.

Just like you wouldn't want to jump out of an airplane without a reserve parachute, if you've got work responsibilities, you shouldn't head out without a backup option of getting online! If you're working or learning remotely over mobile Internet, you simply need multiple ways to get online. Each location will vary in what works best, such as a Jetpack from Verizon with an antenna, a hotspot from AT&T with a booster, or perhaps the RV park's advertised Wi-Fi (hey, good Wi-Fi *might* happen!). When you have a weak signal on one of your options, you need to move to plan B, C, or even D to get online. And when all else fails, be ready to drive into the nearest town to get a whiff of signal.

337   Bring your own Internet connection.

If Internet connectivity is essential to you—whether it's for work, entertainment, or roadschooling your kids—bring your own Wi-Fi solution with you. While many RV parks and campgrounds offer free Internet, it's not always reliable or suitable for streaming. Some have usage limits, and an open public Wi-Fi network isn't secure. Whether you bring your own Wi-Fi Jetpack or MiFi device (these are basically the same thing), or simply use the Personal Hotspot feature on your smartphone, you'll have a better and more consistently reliable online experience.

338   Double or triple your coverage options.

If you rely on the Internet to work as you travel, consider having plans with two or even three major carriers to increase your coverage options. In the US, Verizon, AT&T, and T-Mobile are generally the best nationwide, while Canada uses Bell, Telus, and Rogers. Having separate networks creates redundancy and will provide much greater flexibility and connectivity as you travel. Yes, it will cost more, but this is key to being able to work effectively while exploring the country in your RV.

339   Keep your mobile Internet setup current.

Technology changes rapidly, and if you want to stay connected it pays to stay up to date. If you have more modern cellular equipment, you gain access to your cellular carrier's newest coverage and technology. Data plans are also changing all the time, so it's worthwhile to reassess your setup and consider what changes you may need to make to keep ahead of the curve.

340 **Avoid mixing heavy work days and long driving days.**

If you are working remotely and have scheduled work hours or deliverables, try to avoid planning to arrive at a new location expecting to be immediately productive. Driving days can be tiring if you encounter traffic, bad weather, or a mechanical breakdown. Setting up your new campsite also takes time. And you may find you just simply can't get online at your new location without lots of tweaking. Whenever possible, plan to arrive at least a day before you need to virtually be in the office.

341 **Beware: Cellular boosters can actually slow you down in some locations!**

In fringe signal areas, cellular boosters can sometimes make a world of difference—helping you get online or place a phone call where it might otherwise be nearly impossible. But in moderate or strong signal areas, turning on a booster might actually slow down your Internet speeds, even if it shows increased signal bars on your phone. Sometimes turning on a booster can cut your download speeds in half! Because of this, never leave a booster on all the time. Use one only when you have done a before and after Internet speed test to make sure that it *is* actually helping.

342   Check coverage ahead of time.

If getting online while you travel by RV is critical, then you need to include mobile Internet access into your travel planning. You can check the coverage maps from your cellular provider, or use the Coverage? app to see all carriers at once. It is a good idea to check campground reviews (via the Campendium and RV LIFE apps, for example) for comments about cellular coverage, or call the RV park and ask which networks work best in the campground.

CHERIE VE ARD AND CHRIS DUNPHY OF TECHNOMADIA.COM AND RVMOBILEINTERNET.COM

"Many years ago, we had set up camp in a beautiful field of wildflowers in Colorado. We checked our Internet connection on our two hotspots and decided this would be a great location to get caught up on some work. So we paid for 3 nights of camping and got settled in. An hour later, we got a text message that we had exceeded our domestic roaming allowance on one of our plans and we were being cut off. No problem, we thought; we have redundancy! And we switched to our backup carrier...but then *they* sent us an email that we had exceeded our roaming cap and they were cutting us off too. Now we had no way to get online. Turns out we needed more redundancy *and* a way to better tell where we had native coverage with our cellular data plans. So we fixed both—we now carry data plans on all of the carriers *and* we created an app called Coverage? to see the carrier's coverage maps right on our smartphones. With a bit of travel planning and knowing our gear and plans, we now arrive at new locations confident that we'll be able to get connected and get our work done."

343

Consider a MIMO antenna to boost your signal.

When selecting your mobile Internet setup, it may be tempting to purchase a cellular booster simply because people talk about them and they cost a lot of money, so they must be good, right? While a booster can serve a role in your mobile Internet setup, it may not offer as much as you hope, for the price point. More often than not, a directly connected MIMO (Multiple-Input Multiple-Output) antenna will outperform a booster when it comes to cellular data performance. When connected to a mobile hotspot device or router with antenna ports, they can be a much more cost-effective and powerful signal-enhancing option.

344   **Do big data uploads or downloads overnight to get them done faster.**

If you are in a congested area with slower Internet and have a large file to upload or download, or a software upgrade, schedule it for the middle of the night. Doing this at a time when most people are sleeping and online use is lower in the area will result in faster speeds and reduce the chance of a failure.

345   **Pay attention to campground names for coverage clues.**

When you're looking for a place to stay, pay special attention to the name of the campground and do some additional research on cellular connectivity if the park you plan to stay at has in their name words like *Hidden*, *Valley*, *Canyon*, or *Secret*. Sometimes even when a cellular carrier's coverage map shows you should get cell coverage there, you may find you don't if you end up camping down in a valley or canyon or are separated from the nearby town by a mountain ridge. Check online reviews or call ahead to the campground office and ask them to confirm which cellular carriers work best in the park—if at all!

346 Find a supportive community of other working RVers.

Seek out *Facebook* groups, podcasts, masterminds, account-ability groups, forums, or any way to connect with other RVers working on the road. Working from an RV instead of an office can be lonely, and having a like-minded community to connect with and fall back on—virtually and in person—while you travel will help you feel motivated and supported.

HEATH AND ALYSSA PADGETT OF THERVENTREPRENEUR .COM AND HEATHANDALYSSA.COM

"Our first year as RVers, we didn't know anyone else full-time RVing—at least not in their 20s. And as we grew our businesses from the RV, we felt even more isolated. It felt like no one else was living life like us, so when we ran into roadblocks and hurdles, we had no one to turn to. It took us 2 years to start our RV Entrepreneur *Facebook* group so we could finally bring together people like us. Working on the road is lonely. Without a community to encourage you or support you, it can feel isolating to work alone in your RV all day. When you work in a silo, you get stuck. You do the same things you've always done without feedback, without a mentor to push you, without a mastermind to give you insight, without input from anyone else. And that feedback and input are what help you grow—and keep you sane."

347 Invest in a multicarrier cellular modem.

Did you know most modems purchased from cellular carriers are locked for use only on that carrier? Even if you have them unlocked, they often are lacking in their ability to function properly on other networks. Free yourself from any single carrier by investing in a multicarrier-supported cellular router such as those made by Peplink or Cradlepoint, which can work on all the major carriers and switch among multiple carriers at a switch of a button. This will prevent duplicate spending down the road and give you plenty of flexibility if you need to change carriers in the future.

ERIK AND KALA MCCAULEY OF LIVINLITE.NET AND MOBILEMUSTHAVE.COM

"We started our RV journey back in 2015 and Internet connectivity was our top priority to ensure job security while working remotely. For us, Internet connectivity isn't just about staying close with family; it is our livelihood. We need the Internet to do our jobs. We quickly learned that no single cellular carrier 100 percent covered the areas we traveled. With our backgrounds in technology, we quickly realized the RV-specific solutions were not going to cut it and went for commercial-grade Internet products. With our multi-cellular-capable router, we can use data plans from all the major carriers in a single device, allowing us to pick the one that works best in that area. We then added a cellular roof antenna that was a game changer for letting us get off the beaten path, adding almost 600 percent more cell signal in many situations. This has cut down on our gear clutter while giving us more connectivity options to keep us online. Now we barely think about the Internet while working on the road!"

348 **Use your TV for slideshow entertainment.**

Put your favorite RV travel, camping, or other adventure photos onto a USB stick or an SD card and pop it into the back of your TV. Instead of using up data for online streaming or watching TV, instead run a digital slideshow to revisit and share fun trips with your family and friends. You can even add images of places you want to visit, like a digital vision board to keep them top of mind.

349 **Improve Internet speeds with a rooftop antenna.**

Did you know that every 10 feet of increase in height will nearly double your cellular signal? Moreover, removing obstructions between you and the cellular tower will double your signal again. Increase your cellular signal by up to 600 percent by adding a roof antenna to your mobile Internet setup. By putting your cellular antenna outside, you are removing the need to fight to get signal through your RV's thick insulation and aluminum construction. Most mobile hotspots or mobile routers have antenna ports that will allow you to take advantage of a roof antenna, which will improve your Internet speed and the range you can camp from civilization while still staying connected.

Chapter 6
FAMILIES, KIDS, AND PETS

An RV is a terrific way to travel with a family—you have flexibility, many of the comforts of home, and the freedom to visit so many places your group will love. Of course, moving kids and pets from one spot to another can be tricky—but planning ahead, anticipating issues, and staying open-minded will help make the experience even more enjoyable. These hacks will help you handle everything from kid meltdowns and roadschooling to panicky pets so you can get the show on the road with a smile.

Treat the world as a giant classroom.

350 **Use a white noise machine or app to help your kids sleep.**

Use natural sounds like crickets, the beach, or birds on a white noise machine or app to muffle the sounds you encounter as you travel. This will help your kids settle down and sleep, and can cover up the sounds of parents who may be staying up later.

351 **Fasten glow stick bracelets on kids to make them more visible at night.**

Put glow stick bracelets on your kids at dusk or after dark so you can more easily see and keep track of them. It is fun for the kids while offering extra peace of mind for parents.

352 **Use a glow stick as a nightlight.**

Hang a glow stick near your child's sleeping spot as a dim nightlight. Some have flexible shapes that make them easy to bend and secure, and the different colors will make your RVing adventure a bit more fun than a regular nightlight would.

353 **Leave a nightlight on.**

Keep a nightlight on in the bathroom so kids and parents don't need to turn on the main lights at night, possibly waking up everyone else in the small space of an RV.

354 **Power outdoor decorative lights with sunlight.**

Hang solar string lights to bring extra light to your evenings without the need for electricity or batteries. These are especially handy when camping without hookups. They bring a nice, soft ambience to your campsite while providing enough light to help young kids feel more secure in unfamiliar environments.

◄ *US 101, Florence, Oregon / Photo © Julie Bennett*

355   Swap wooden sticks for metal skewers for safer toasting.

When toasting marshmallows, use telescoping metal skewers instead of wooden sticks. These keep kids farther away from the fire and safer from unpredictable sparks. The hot metal can also heat the marshmallow from the inside, making it soft and gooey without overcooking the outside, plus they pack down nice and compactly.

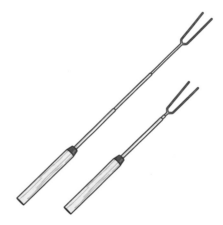

356   Use a wire hanger to toast food.

In a pinch, wire coat hangers can be unwound and turned into a long skewer for roasting hot dogs or marshmallows.

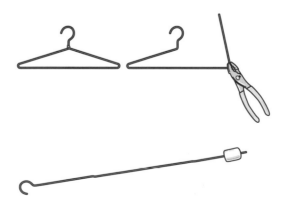

357 Get the wiggles out.

Plan to stop frequently when traveling long distances with kids to get out the wiggles and keep them (and you) happy. This means a little extra travel planning, but it is worth it. The last thing you want to be doing on a family road trip is having to take a random exit with no plan to pull over your rig safely, especially with bigger RVs. Taking the extra time to plan rest stops and meal breaks will result in a much more pleasant experience for all. Try to plan for stops at a local park and even have a picnic along the way.

KALI AND JOSH SPIERS OF THE FREEDOM THEORY ON *YOUTUBE*

"When we hit the road with our firstborn son, Landyn, it was tough adapting to his style of travel. Unlike some littles, we learned Landyn wasn't born with an immediate travel bug or a love for his car seat. We were all a bit miserable trying to figure out how to make it work and keep everyone happy on our RVing adventures. After lots of trial and error, we started planning to make stops every hour. Now we have two toddlers, and we find if the kids are doing well, we can skip a stop. But if things are getting dicey, we know we have a plan and a place to get off the road safely. This has helped us see so many things we may have otherwise missed on our travels, and saved us from countless meltdowns in the car."

358 Create a makeshift bathtub for littles.

Most RVs don't have bathtubs or big sinks, so use a plastic storage bin or an inflatable baby bath as a makeshift tub to bathe young kids, then just dump the water down the shower drain when done.

359 Buy RVs for you, not occasional guests.

Don't make your RV purchasing decisions based around hosting occasional guests, like grandkids, who may not visit as often as you'd like. You can always use an inflatable air mattress, or an above-cab drop-down bunk that can be stowed away or used as storage when not in use. You can even get a tent so they can combine their stay with a fun outdoor adventure at your campsite. If you are doing extended RV travel, buy the RV that meets your own personal needs at least 90 percent of the time.

360 Camp in kid-friendly locations.

When traveling with kids, choose a campground that offers kid-focused activities. This will also attract other families and keep kids more easily entertained, giving parents time for themselves to relax, and ensure you all have a good experience. You can also try boondocking in locations like national forests and other free public lands so the kids can get out and explore, connect with nature, and make noise without having to worry about nearby neighbors in a campground.

361 Keep your dinette cushion covers clean.

Use crib sheets as covers for dinette cushions. These are quick and easy to wash and change if your kids spill anything, and you can use different colors to freshen up the look of your RV decor.

362

Know your state's home-schooling laws.

Planning to travel extensively and road-school your kids? Get the right information before you hit the highway and visit the Home School Legal Defense Association website (https://hslda.org) to check on regulations and requirements for your state. There you will also find education resources, planning tools, curriculums, tests, and support groups, plus resources for kids with special needs.

363 Approach schooling in a flexible way.

After being on the road for more than 6 years, roadschooling four kids, our top tip is to be flexible! Being on the road presents so many great learning opportunities. Don't be stuck to a rigid school schedule. Instead, let it ebb and flow based on your travels. The kids learn a ton just being out in nature, hiking, exploring, and playing with other kids around the campground!

BRYANNA ROYAL, CRAZYFAMILYADVENTURE.COM AND AUTHOR OF *FULL-TIME RVING WITH KIDS*

"The knowledge we have seen our kids gain from spending a day exploring a national park is unbelievable. You can't write a curriculum that has you seeing a momma bear walk across the road with her cubs or watching a pack of wolves chase down an elk for their daily meal. What our kids have learned from these experiences—when we left the books and worksheets behind and went out exploring and adventuring—is unreal. Our oldest began learning how to read by reading signs to us in national parks. They have also learned about redwoods and sequoias by reading about them, hugging them, and climbing them! Our national and state parks do an amazing job with their visitor centers and junior ranger programs. Roadschooling to us is all about exploring, adventuring, and learning as we go. We don't have a set curriculum or schedule but instead adjust to our day based on where we are and our surroundings. When our kids see, touch, smell, and feel what they are learning, it is all being absorbed at such a deeper level. I am so glad that we have given our kids this experience of learning from the road!"

364 Use snack food as a motivational tool.

There's no denying snacks and treats can be an excellent motivator for kids. When it comes to taking kids out for a long hike or other big adventure, pack some favorite snacks and treats that you know will excite them. It will keep their energy up and help avoid getting hangry, potentially spoiling what could have been a fun event. Make sure you bring plenty of water as well and even an energy drink to keep them well hydrated, especially in hot weather.

STEPHANIE AND JEREMY PUGLISI OF *THE RV ATLAS* PODCAST AND AUTHORS OF *SEE YOU AT THE CAMPGROUND* AND *WHERE SHOULD WE CAMP NEXT?*

"Food is the ultimate coping tool, so my favorite gear for having adventures with kids is bringing lots of snacks. I was the mom that used to make my own baby food, but when it comes to getting kids motivated for a hike or big adventure, we look at the big picture. We figure they are burning off the calories anyway, so a few less healthy treats are OK and make it more fun for our boys. As long as we remember to bring plenty of food and snacks along on our big days out, we always have a great time!"

365 Expand your space with a large patio mat.

Carrying a big patio mat helps expand your RV living space and gives kids a place to set up and play outside while staying close by so you can keep an eye on them. A patio mat will also help reduce the amount of dust and dirt being tracked into your RV, keeping the kids and your RV interior somewhat cleaner.

366 **Treat the world as a giant classroom.**

Fast-track and enhance your kids' learning through real-life experiences. Use paper maps to plan routes. Practice math by tracking mile markers along your hike or route. Observe the terrain and plants in a changing environment. Notice the different accents and languages of people from other countries. Find educational opportunities in museums and national and state parks. Explore national forests. Make the most of each location you visit by seeking out opportunities to create a more immersive and memorable environment for your kids to become more curious and to learn and grow as you travel.

367 **Do a practice run with gear at home.**

Instead of learning how to use new gear like boots, backpacks, and hiking poles while out on a camping trip, do a trial run with your kids at home in your yard or in a nearby park before going on a long-distance trip. The kids will feel more comfortable with the gear if it isn't their first time, which can minimize complaining. And your own practice will make you more efficient in setup and ensure you have everything you need before you leave.

368 **Combine evening walks with a flashlight scavenger hunt.**

When you're camped, plan for a nighttime scavenger hunt to entertain kids while taking an evening walk. Hide small toys, animal figures, or treats in and around your campsite in the daytime. Then take your flashlights along for an evening family walk after dinner. The search and discovery game can be fun and exciting for kids, and the flashlights will help keep them entertained for much longer than if they were searching in full daylight. This is a good activity to tire the kids out before bed.

▶ *Garden of the Gods RV Resort, Colorado Springs, Colorado / Photo © Julie Bennett*

Do a practice run
with gear at home.

369 Schedule your trip around kids' normal routines.

An RV allows you to bring more of your home life and schedule with you than a plane trip, as it's a more consistent and controlled environment. So create some structure in your schedule and balance adventure time versus downtime. Keep the same mealtimes, nap times, and sleep schedules that you have at home to keep a healthy, happy balance between your vacation life and home life. If your kids are better in the mornings, try to plan the biggest events of the day—whether it's their schooling, a hike, or other adventure—in the morning. If you try to plan things to happen around what would normally be nap time, you're bound to have challenges.

370 Respect and plan for downtime.

Everyone needs time to just chill, and camping trips are great for having downtime without getting bored. It can be fun to just hang out at your RV or around the campground. By all means, go out and do your adventuring and high-energy activities, but always plan for time to wind down—whether it's relaxing by the pool, playing games, or sitting by the campfire.

371 Buy quality secondhand outdoor gear.

Having the right gear and equipment can make all the difference, but you don't need to buy new! You can often find gently used, high-quality equipment (backpacks, child carriers, off-road running strollers, etc.) on *Facebook Marketplace*, *Craigslist*, or *eBay*. You will spend less money on lightly used, high-quality gear than new, lower-quality gear that may not work as well or last as long. If you buy the good-quality stuff, you will have a better experience. You may even be able to resell it later if the kids outgrow the gear or if it turns out it's not used as much as you expected.

372 **Put up a shade shelter.**

Bring a foldable pop-up shade shelter or beach tent to create a dedicated space for kids to play in outside at the campsite. A shelter tent helps contain the kids' play space and toys while reducing their exposure to the sun, which means fewer sunscreen reapplications! It also creates some separation, giving parents their own space to relax outside. These tent shelters can be great for your campsite, and they're portable enough to take on other adventures, like a trip to the beach or lake.

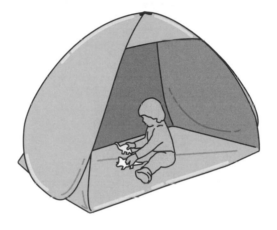

373

Connect with other families.

Contrary to what you may think, RV life doesn't have to be lonely. In fact, it can be extremely social! Meet other families in camp-grounds. Join groups like Worldschoolers on *Facebook* and Fulltime Families (www.full timefamilies.com) to connect and participate in family-focused RV events. Caravan with another RV family or two so you always have company, playmates, and support along the way.

374 **Get a money-saving reciprocal pass for science centers.**

Sign up your family for a nationwide pass of reciprocal benefits to more than 150 zoos and aquariums and 300 science centers worldwide through the Association of Zoos and Aquariums (AZA) and Association of Science and Technology Centers (ASTC) reciprocal programs. This is an affordable way for the whole family to stretch their legs while offering fun learning opportunities. Make sure to call ahead and verify partnership and availability of RV parking if you'll be visiting with your rig in tow. It makes a great gift idea for your kids each year. Visit www.astc.org and www.aza.org to learn more.

MARISSA AND NATHAN MOSS OF LESSJUNKMOREJOURNEY .COM

"Traveling with kids is one of the most rewarding yet challenging experiences as a parent. Our children were the inspiration for us to start camping as a family and making incredible memories together. The most impactful hack for us traveling with children is allowing time for them to stretch their legs in fun, interactive ways. Once we discovered the difference it made to stop at a park for a picnic lunch or break up the travel day with a visit to an aquarium or science museum, it helped make our children more patient travelers. One of the biggest money savers we discovered during one of these stops was purchasing a nationwide access pass we could use at certain places as we traveled. You can buy a yearly pass that provides free admission or discounted rates for the whole family at participating science museums, zoos, aquariums, and even children's museums. Many of these programs are reciprocal, and the pass is fun for all ages and has been a lifesaver, as well as money saver, for traveling with children."

375 Create a makeshift toilet for nighttime use.

If your RV doesn't have a toilet or you are tent camping, create a small makeshift toilet to use at night, so you—and particularly your kids—don't have to walk to public bathhouses in the middle of the night, especially if it's a long walk, if it's cold or rainy, or if there's wildlife in the area. Keeping a small bucket with a lid for nighttime bathroom visits will make for easy, no-spill transporting when you dump the bucket at the public restroom the next morning.

376 Involve your kids in every aspect of RV life.

Enlist your kids to help plan your RV camping trips, do research, navigate, set up camp, cook, clean, budget, and meet camping neighbors. These are the real-life skills they will need to be happy and successful adults anyway!

377 Take learning to the library.

Libraries can be great places to do some focused learning if you're roadschooling your kids. They create some separation from the RV, and while in a library, kids need to stay quiet and focused on their assignments. And most libraries offer free Wi-Fi too.

378 Choose foldable, stowable, durable gear.

Babies may be tiny, but they need quite a few things, especially when traveling. You may want a high chair, stroller, playpen, travel bed for co-sleeping, body carrier, and/or baby bath. You'll want to choose gear that can be easily stowed when it's not in use, like a foldable high chair. An inflatable baby bathtub can fit in any RV shower, making bath time so much easier.

379 Look for RVs that can secure a car seat.

Keeping babies and small children safe while traveling in an RV is a huge concern for many parents—especially if you plan on traveling in a motorhome. This is less of an issue if you're towing a trailer and you can safely latch your car seat into your vehicle. But motorhomes may not necessarily have forward-facing seats or a LATCH system. This is something to consider before you buy or rent an RV. You'll want to find a motorhome with a dinette booth that has LATCH or additional anchors installed. In order to secure a bulky car seat into your dinette booth, you may want to lower the table into the bed position so it fits. The lowered table is also a great place to store a toy bin or snacks for the drive so they are within easy reach.

ALYSSA PADGETT OF THERVENTREPRENEUR.COM AND HEATHANDALYSSA.COM

"On our first RV trip with our daughter, we rented an RV in Italy. The RV rental company offered front-facing car seats, but since she was only 4 months old, we had to bring our own rear-facing car seat. I assumed the RV could fit a car seat since the company rented them, but I never thought to ask about the dimensions! So after flying halfway across the world, we went to secure our car seat and it wouldn't fit! Luckily, the cushions in the dinette were able to be removed so we could safely install the seat there. In the future, I'll always ask for measurements when we rent an RV!"

A well-socialized dog will do best on the road.

380 **Keep some things special for RV trips only.**

RVs are great for being able to bring along things from home for the kids, like a familiar blanket or crib. But it can also be helpful to have a few special items, like books or toys, that are *only* for your RV camping trips. This helps keep the RV experiences special and different from home, enhancing the memories tied to the RV.

381 **Create individual storage areas for kids.**

Mount a bookshelf, basket, or hanging cubby at the foot of the bed for each kid so they have their own area for clothes and toys.

382 **Warm up to first-time RVing for your pet.**

If your pet gets nervous about traveling, be proactive and work slowly on getting them used to the RV. This is especially important for a motorhome, as they make noises going down the road and sometimes things fall and make a noise, which can scare pets. As you are setting up your RV, invite your pet to hang with you in the RV. Give them treats and chews, and feed them all in the RV. Play games with their favorite toys, run through their tricks, and deliver lots of treats. Don't start rolling down the road until your pet can lie down inside the RV and be totally comfortable in it. And when you do get going, start out with a short trip. Shakedown trips to your local campground are always a good idea so you can see how your pet does and what supplies you need to gather for the next adventure.

◄ *Pacific City Beach, Cape Kiwanda State Natural Area, Oregon / Photo © Julie Bennett*

383   **Keep a window partially open for fresh air to expose your pet to new smells.**

While driving, keep the window open just enough to bring in new smells for your dog. This will keep them interested, and fresh air helps if they are prone to motion sickness. But don't open the window all the way. While your dog may like it and it can make for a fun photo, it's also a safety hazard, as they could jump or fall out, or be hit with flying road debris.

384   **Combat canine motion sickness.**

Some dogs can get anxious in the car, and may even be prone to motion sickness. While you can give them motion-sickness drugs, holistic vets say dog owners should consider natural alternatives. These natural remedies can create a more relaxing atmosphere that will soothe your pup (and even passengers). For example: 1) Apply a few drops of lavender or chamomile oil to a cotton ball and place it inside the vehicle about 30 minutes before your departure in order to fill the vehicle with a soothing aroma. (Remove the cotton ball so your dog doesn't eat it!). 2) Crate your dog to keep them looking ahead. 3) For long drives, buy a soup bone at the grocery store. Your dog will be focused on chewing the bone during the ride and won't even notice they're in the car.

385   **Be mindful before and during slideout closings.**

Make sure your pets are safely in a pet carrier or securely tethered outside the RV when bringing in slideout rooms so they don't get scared or squashed. Seeing and hearing the moving walls might scare them and make them feel less safe in the RV environment in general. And keep an eye on your cats, as they like to hide in secret places, which may involve slideouts!

386   Know how to find a lost pet while RVing.

If you lose your pet while RVing away from home, first contact the local animal control and animal shelters. These are often the first places people will take them. Secondly, call the local vet clinics in case they are brought in there. If you don't get any leads from these sources, post in local *Facebook* groups. And *Facebook* ads allow you to pay to target a post to a particular geographic area. To do that, create a *Facebook* business account to access the Ads feature. Then build your "ad" with a photo of your lost pet and your contact information. This will reach many more people far more quickly than posting flyers.

CAITLIN AND TOM MORTON OF MORTONSONTHE MOVE.COM

"We travel full-time with our two dogs, Mocha and Bella. One of our biggest concerns was one of them wandering off and getting lost. One day, our nightmare came true. Bella escaped from the car while we were running errands. When we came back, she was gone without a trace. She was wearing a collar, but had lost her ID tags, and we hadn't yet replaced them. We searched the area for hours. Then, my husband Tom had the idea of posting an ad to *Facebook* and paying to get it in front of everyone in the county. We already had a *Facebook* business account, so we quickly built and launched a 'Lost Dog' ad. Not only did the ad appear for people in the local area, but those people then shared it within their town-based *Facebook* Groups and local animal shelters. Within 9 minutes our 'Lost Dog' ad had been seen by over ten thousand people, and we had four different people texting us that they'd seen a post of a found dog that looked like Bella. Within 15 minutes, we were on the phone with the lady who had found her. Once our $50 ad got out into the community, so many kind-hearted people enthusiastically shared it to help us find our Bella!"

387 Put in a pet door or ramp.

Modify your RV to install a pet door or even a built-in ramp through one of the basement bays. If your RV floor plan allows you to access an exterior basement storage area from inside the RV, try this handy solution. Install a pet door where the RV interior and basement meet. Then keep the exterior basement storage door securely propped open and install a ramp from the storage bay to the ground so your pet can come and go as they please. Of course, you'll need a good foldable fence area at the base so they remain on your campsite. If your pet has difficulty climbing the often steep, open, and slippery steps to your RV entry door, you can build a front entry ramp for them to make it easier to get in and out of the RV entry door.

388 **Build a custom crate to fit.**

If your dog likes to sleep in a crate, make a built-in custom crate under a booth dinette seat or under the bed. It will save on your RV floor space while giving them their own. Depending on the size of your dog, it may mean your dinette seats or bed sit a little higher than normal, but this will be more space efficient than trying to make room for traditional, full-sized crates. You can also use the lower part of an RV bunk area for pet crates or to build a kennel.

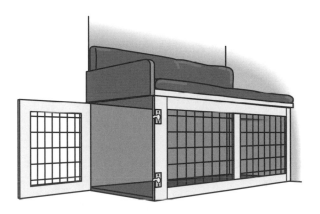

389 **Take your kitties for a walk too!**

If your cat is used to being outside, you will want to get them accustomed to a harness and leash. Start this inside your home and in your home outdoor space. Try a few minutes first and work up to more time gradually each day. Outside your RV, always be with your cat on the leash for safety. Be mindful of what is around you, like dogs.

390 **Save your floors from pet claws.**

Use a rubber-backed runner rug in high-traffic areas of your RV to reduce wear and tear, especially if you have pets that like to run up and down the main area when excited.

391   Make time for doggy school.

Brush up on your dog's skills with some basic training and commands like *Sit, Stay, Come,* and *Wait.* Make sure they are getting out of your house or yard to other areas like parks and that they're going on walks. And if they like other dogs, then take them to dog parks. A well-socialized dog will do best on the road, so each week, take your dog somewhere new, like a coffee shop, to get them used to meeting other people and changing environments. Practice your basic commands so when you are out RV camping, your dog will respond quickly.

392   Keep your dog cool in the heat.

In hot weather, inside or out, use a spray mist bottle of clean water to moisten your dog's coat, or place a damp towel over them to help them cool off.

393   Keep dog beds away from gas detectors to avoid false alarms.

If you're traveling with pets, especially dogs, avoid placing their doggy bed—and letting them lie next to—the gas detector. A dog with digestive issues may fart and emit enough methane to set off your RV's propane/natural gas detector. Not only can this wake you with a scare in the middle of the night; without knowing this can happen, you might spend hours worrying you have a more serious problem with a propane leak when the fix can be as simple as moving the dog away from the sensor.

394

Keep your dog anchored with a cable.

Use a leash anchor and cable to allow your pet to hang out with you outside without needing to constantly hold their leash. Store their leash right by the RV door and keep the end of their outside anchor cable next to the door so that you can attach the cable before you let them out.

395 Create a kitty litter cabinet.

Wondering where to hide your kitty litter box? Remove your lower bathroom cabinet door and place your cat litter box inside, then hang a small curtain in place of the door to hide it. This keeps it out of the way and provides a great little private spot for your cat to do their business. And you can leave the ceiling vent in the bathroom open for extra ventilation.

396 Utilize a storage bay for your litter box.

If your RV floor plan allows it, create a kitty passage door down into an exterior storage bay. This will ventilate the area more easily to the outside, while also providing easy access for cleaning and changing the kitty litter from the outside. Just make sure the outside basement door is secure so your cat can't get out (unless it's an outside cat, of course).

397 **Put a water bowl in the shower area to reduce spills and save space.**

Keep your pet's water bowl in the shower to reduce spills and mess, and save floor space in your main living area.

398 **Run before you hit the road.**

Before heading out on a long road trip, take your dog out for a long exercise run first. When they are tired, they will rest better during travel.

399 **Install an automated generator starter to keep pets safe.**

Many motorhomes, and some large trailers, have onboard generators to power their RV house systems when they are not plugged into electricity. Most RVs are not well insulated, so inside temperatures can vary significantly, in summer and winter, if you are not running the air conditioner or heater. If you sometimes leave your pet alone in the RV, you might want to install an automated generator starter (commonly referred to as an autogen). This system allows your RV to automatically start the generator if there is a power outage and your RV gets too hot or cold, or if your RV is not plugged into power while camping off the grid. This will provide you with peace of mind, knowing your pets are safe and comfortable when they are home alone in the RV.

Seven Tips for Traveling with Pets

400 Add your current location to your pet's tags.

In addition to the pet's usual tags and/or chip, add a temporary tag for where you are staying. Pick up write-on tags—the little white round tags with metal on the rim. Write the name of the campground and your RV site number on it.

401 Be prepared for the unexpected.

Gather copies of shot records and pertinent medical records for all pets that you are traveling with. Keep these in your vehicle. That way if you need an emergency veterinary clinic, you are ready with the information you'll need. Some RV parks may also ask for your pet's shot records.

402 Keep them tethered.

Keep your pet on a leash or securely anchored anytime you are outside of confined environments (like your RV or a dog park).

403 Vaccinate pets before vacation.

When you're trip planning, ensure all pets have the required vaccinations for the areas you'll be traveling. This is extra important if you're planning an international border crossing.

404 Train pets to wait.

Train your pets to wait so they know to stay inside the RV until it is safe and you give the okay to leave so they don't unexpectedly run out the door in new places.

405 Avoid driver seat distraction.

Keep pets secured while driving so they can't access the driver's area while the vehicle is in motion.

406 Check campground pet policies in advance.

Some campgrounds have restrictions on the breed, type, or number of pets traveling with you, so ask when making reservations.

407 **Fence in pets.**

Use a baby gate or foldable gates at your RV entry door to make a small fenced-in area outside on your RV patio. This allows you to keep your main entry door open for light and fresh air, and your pet can enjoy the outside while staying contained and safe.

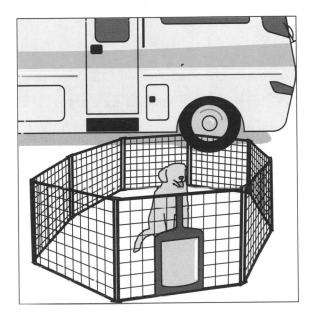

408 **Contain that pup.**

It's important that your dog stay on your campsite, so consider getting an exercise pen. These are metal folding fences used by many RVers that fold up flat and come in different heights. Several pens may be needed to create an adequate-sized area for you and your dogs. They can be really great for those whose dog will respect the fence and not knock it down and also those with RVs who have the storage space. But note that some RV parks do not allow these.

409

Teach cats to travel in crates.

If you travel with a cat, keeping a pet carrier in your vehicle or motorhome is essential. Start having your cat spend time in the crate in your home, then progress up to having the cat in the carrier in the vehicle when not moving. Then take some short drives, comforting your cat along the way with your voice. If your cat likes treats, make sure they get some while in the crate.

410   Tag and chip your pets.

It's so important to always have a collar or harness with ID tags that have your current phone number on your pet. This collar/harness should remain on your pet 24/7 when traveling. This way, if they accidentally do get away from you for any reason, they have ID on them. Carry at least two extra tags in your car in case they fall off while traveling. Many hardware stores and chain pet supply stores can make these in-house. And, of course, microchipping is another way to identify your pet and have them returned to you if lost. A microchip can be scanned and read at a vet clinic, animal shelter, or animal control facility.

411   Remove pet hair.

In a small space, pet hair can build up fast and is extremely noticeable. Bottom line: You need to remove it, almost daily. Get a small rechargeable stick vacuum like a Dyson that is compact and easy to access.

412   Consider a crate for dogs while moving.

If your dog is anxious or young, you might want to have a crate in your motorhome or vehicle. Start by introducing them to the crate in your home. Feed your pup in the crate, and give them toys and chews while in the crate. Make it a "happy place" for the dog. Try short sessions starting at 5 minutes and increasing the time to work up to an hour or so. If your dog looks at the crate as a pleasant place to be, it will make for a much more pleasant experience for all when the vehicle is moving.

413
Make a stop just before you arrive at campgrounds to let your dogs out for a bit.

About 30 minutes to an hour before reaching your final destination, schedule a stop. Get out and walk your dogs and let them have a good sniff and potty break. You too! Get a snack or have a meal. That way, when you reach your RV park, the dogs will be less anxious about getting out, and you can take your time setting up your RV.

JULIET WHITFIELD OF TAILSFROMTHEROAD.COM

"After many times arriving at RV parks with hysterical dogs wanting to get out and me getting hangry, one day I decided to stop about half an hour before my destination. I took the dogs for a walk, we all went potty and stretched our legs, and I ate some lunch. Soon after, when I arrived at the RV park, I realized my dogs were relaxed and not so anxious to get out. I was able to get the RV set up, then take them outside, and it was a much calmer experience for all of us. This made such a huge difference for my dogs that I now make this extra scheduled stop on any long trip."

414
Choose small solutions to big pet problems.

If typical pet products don't fit in your RV, look for other solutions. For example, is your litter box too big for your RV? Get a smaller clear plastic bin like those available at most of the big-box retailers. They come in much smaller sizes than a regular kitty litter box yet are still big enough for your cat to do its business. Meanwhile, you won't be losing half your floor space. These plastic bins also come with a lid for travel day, which makes cleanup or storing much easier than with a traditional litter box.

415 **Pick up dog hair without a vacuum.**

Wipe over the furniture or carpet using a slightly damp shower squeegee or rubber glove to pick up a surprising amount of fur.

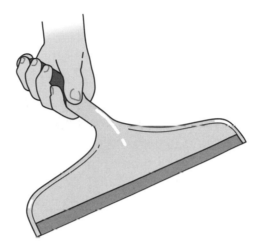

CONCLUSION

If there's one thing we've learned about RV life over the years, it's that you never stop learning! There's always a new opportunity to find a way to do something better. To save time or money. Or get yourself out of a pickle. But, for us, the best part of learning about or coming up with new hacks is sharing them with others. We hope you picked up a ton of new tips and tricks to make your RV life easier, safer, and more fun! Now it's time to get out there and put them into practice!

Happy travels! Best of life,

—Marc and Julie

PS. Thanks so much for reading. If you enjoyed this book, please consider leaving an honest review at your favorite online store.

Want even more RV hacks?

Jump over to our website: **www.RVLove.com/Bonus Hacks**. There, you'll also find a handy summary of the links we shared in this book, plus some discount codes that can save you money too.

Got an RV hack of your own you'd like to share?

We'd love to hear about it! Submit your hack at **www.RVLove.com/BonusHacks**.

Discover more articles and videos, get free downloads, and find even more resources to help you in your RV life at **RVLove.com**.

Want to stay in touch?

Here are ways we can connect:

- Check out our website:
  www.RVLove.com

- Sign up for our email updates:
  www.RVLove.com/email-sign-up

- Watch our videos on *YouTube*:
  www.youtube.com/RVLoveTV

- Like us on *Facebook*:
  www.facebook.com/RVLoveTV

- Follow us on *Instagram*:
  www.instagram.com/RVLoveTravel

- Check out our Pins on *Pinterest*:
  www.pinterest.com/RVLoveTravel

- Connect with us on *Twitter*:
  www.twitter.com/RVLoveTravel

- Find more RV Resources & Discount Codes:
  www.RVLove.com/Resources

- Learn about all of our books: **www.RVLove.com/Books**

INDEX